SOUTH ISLAND
weekend tramps

NICK GROVES

CRAIG
POTTON
PUBLISHING

To Robbie and the next generation, who I hope will continue
to find pleasure in the natural world.

Filmwork: Image Centre Ltd, Auckland, New Zealand
Printed by Everbest Printing Co. Ltd, China

First published in 2003 by Craig Potton Publishing
98 Vickerman Street, PO Box 555, Nelson, New Zealand
www.craigpotton.co.nz

© Craig Potton Publishing
© Text and photographs: Nick Groves
ISBN 1-877333-04-2

ACKNOWLEDGEMENTS

This book would not have happened without the help and encouragement of a wide range of people who thought it a most worthwhile project.

In particular, I'd like to thank my son, Robbie Groves, who joined me on a number of the tramps, but who also put up with a very absent father during the researching of this book. Second, special thanks go to Boel from Sweden, my hiking companion, who encouraged me to get out and complete many of the final summer's trips to some great and memorable places.

A lot of other friends have provided necessary advice and good company on these tramps over the years, namely Shaun Barnett, Tina Becker, Rosie Black, Jutta, Thea and Rowan Blank, Mark Brabyn and willing models on Hiking New Zealand tours, James Broadbent, Rob Brown, Clare Dunston, Carolyn Hewlett, Simon Johnson, Andrew Lynch, John Marcussen, Christina Van Mierlo, Johnny Mulheron, Don Richardson, Jenny Sandblom, Hanna Suckling, Mike White, Zoe De Wit and Simon Young.

Neville Jones of Mapworld in Christchurch provided a very useful CD-ROM of the South Island's 1:50,000 series, plus discounted maps.

Individuals at various Department of Conservation (DoC) offices and visitor centres have added their input, and I must acknowledge the excellent DoC track pamphlets that, along with existing tramping guidebooks by Sven Brabyn and Mark Pickering (see 'References and Further Reading', page 11), all helped considerably in the writing of this book.

Also, many thanks to Anna Parkin of Oxted, England for the use of her computer during the final checks of this book.

Last but by no means least, coffees, meals and music up and down the length of the South Island were kindly provided by Cathy and Ad Sintenie and family of Geraldine, by Christina and Dean Van Mierlo of Punakaiki, and by many others too numerous to mention.

Thanks to everyone else who helped along the way!

CONTENTS

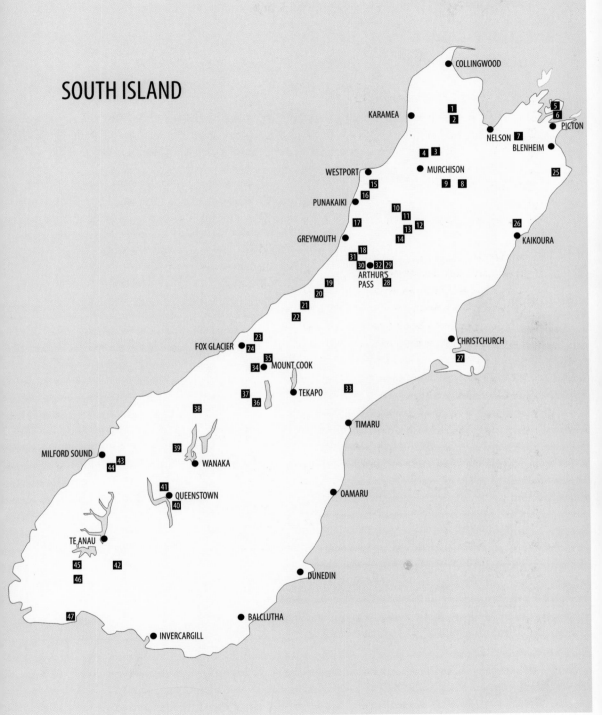

SOUTH ISLAND

COLLINGWOOD

KARAMEA

1
2

5
6
PICTON

NELSON
7
BLENHEIM

4 3

WESTPORT

MURCHISON

9 8

25

15

PUNAKAIKI

16

10

11 12

26

17

13

KAIKOURA

GREYMOUTH

14

18

31

30 32 29

ARTHUR'S
PASS

28

19

20

21

22

CHRISTCHURCH

23

FOX GLACIER

24

27

35

34 MOUNT COOK

37

33

36

TEKAPO

38

TIMARU

MILFORD SOUND

39

43

44

WANAKA

41

QUEENSTOWN

40

OAMARU

TE ANAU

45

42

46

DUNEDIN

47

BALCLUTHA

INVERCARGILL

INTRODUCTION

I was approached back in the spring of 2000 by Rob Brown, who suggested I write a book on tramps suitable for weekenders based in the South Island. He provided a list of about 50 trips and left me to walk and photograph them, having informed Craig Potton Publishing that a writer had been found. Over the ensuing two-and-a-half years, this list saw many changes, additions and rejections as I researched Te Wai Pounamu for the perfect balance of trips to excite every aspiration and ability. I aimed for a blend of popular trips, which everyone would expect to be included in such a guidebook, along with some more obscure yet equally rewarding places to stimulate and encourage forays into these less well-known areas. As Shaun Barnett was already working on the North Island volume, I was aware that I had taken on a challenge to write a companion volume for the South.

When I began the project, it soon became apparent to me that my knowledge of the many wonderful regions of the South Island was in need of improvement. Since my background has always been that of a mountaineer rather than a tramper, I had only walked 15 of the long list of tramps Rob Brown had suggested. Writing this book therefore opened my eyes to the fabulous wealth of natural environments in the South Island that lie within relatively easy reach of our main centres of population.

The 'weekend' concept has been stretched to three days (i.e. a holiday weekend!) for a number of these tramps, although in many cases those with limited time at their disposal can still complete them in a normal weekend. The Queen Charlotte Track is the only longer trip and was included because of the ease with which sections can be walked, or cycled, over an average weekend.

Some of the tramps are, by necessity, in remoter regions of the island and will require a long drive to reach from the main towns and cities. Even so, let's not forget that people living in Te Anau and Hokitika can also be limited to weekend trips away! Our good road network and modern vehicles mean that nowhere is beyond the reach of a suitably enthusiastic 'weekend warrior'; even though I have a 20-year-old Toyota and am based in Lyttelton, I did many of these tramps in the allotted time frame. For example, the last two routes I walked, in June 2003 – Mt Fox on the West Coast and Mt Richmond near Blenheim – were completed over the two days, utilising the Friday evening for the drive to the mountains.

I have also tried to cover a variety of South Island landscapes in the book. Most of the trips are in either national parks or forest parks and vary from dense rainforest to sweeping tussock tops and permanently snow-covered passes and minor summits. From the distinctive marble mountains of Kahurangi National Park in the north to the rough, ice-hewn granite peaks of Fiordland, and from the intimate forested gorges of the Paparoas to the flower-strewn uplands of the West Coast, with views to the highest peaks, there is something for everyone who is prepared to make the effort to head to the hills.

LENGTH AND DIFFICULTY

Each tramp is classified according to difficulty, which readers should note depends very much on conditions. Wet weather could very well turn a medium river trip into a hard, or even impossible one, while winter snow may transform a medium or hard tops trip into one that requires mountaineering skills. When selecting a tramp it is important to take the abilities of all party members into consideration.

Each walk is classified into 'easy', 'moderate' or 'hard', with a few gradings such as 'rock scrambling', 'route-finding skills' and 'easy mountaineering' to cover specific difficulties. On an 'easy' walk you can expect gentle terrain, well-marked tracks, few if any river crossings and walking times of usually three to four (but occasionally more) hours per day. Expect a cosy hut at the end of the first day on two-day 'easy' trips, enabling packs to be kept lighter. On a 'moderate' trip you may have river crossings, and there could be steep sections of track over slippery rocks, mud and tree roots, as well as travel on unmarked, open tops. Some days can be quite long at this grade; on occasions, expect eight hours tramping or more, depending on how you have planned the trip. A 'hard' tramp may involve even longer days, but more usually this grade reflects the rugged nature of the terrain, with route-finding difficulties and long stretches of unmarked travel above the bushline or short sections across snowfields.

The main difference with the choice of trips in this volume compared with those in the North Island book is the inclusion of several above-snowline excursions. Of the 47 tramps described, eight require the competent use of ice axes and crampons in order to travel safely over the permanent snowfields or minor glaciers that are encountered at the higher elevations. The skills to travel safely across such terrain open up a wealth of possibilities for the South Island tramper, as there are innumerable side trips to snow-covered peaks. In addition, early season trips can be undertaken safely as winter snow often lingers on shadier slopes until after Christmas. There are a number of short courses run by experienced instructors that teach these vital skills; in my opinion, this would be money well spent.

The majority of the trips chosen for this book are, however, of moderate difficulty, with a smaller percentage at both ends of the scale, from easy to hard trips. There is therefore something for everyone, with the chance to extend yourself as your experience develops.

KEEPING INFORMATION UP TO DATE

Although every effort has been made to keep the information in this guide both correct and up to date, please remember that nothing stays the same in the outdoors. Landslides, floods or even earthquakes can damage or destroy facilities such as tracks and bridges, while a carelessly abandoned fireplace can soon reduce a backcountry hut to ashes. As I write this, Flora Hut in Kahurangi National Park has sadly just been vandalised.

In addition, the condition of less frequently visited tracks may deteriorate if underused, which is one reason I have included a few out-of-the-way places in order to encourage their continuing maintenance or even an eventual improvement of facilities.

It is always a good idea to call in at the local Department of Conservation (DoC) offices for the latest updates; their phone numbers are included with every tramp.

MAPS

Each tramp in this book is accompanied by a map to help the reader follow the track description. The base maps are digital images created by Roger Smith, the director of GeographX, a Wellington-based company that specialises in advanced digital mapping (for more information, refer to *Landforms – The Shaping of the New Zealand*; see 'Further Reading', page 11). Drawn over these topographically accurate maps are the relevant tracks, huts, bridges and major features referred to in the route descriptions. The maps are not, however, designed to be used for navigation in the outdoors.

For all of the tramps in this book, the correct NZMS 260 series 1:50,000 map(s) should be purchased, not only for reasons of safety but also for the pleasure of being able to identify correctly prominent features along the way. With regard to this, it is worth noting that the inclusion of neighbouring maps to the one specific for the tramp may prove a bonus – as I learnt the hard way. While enjoying a particularly spectacular evening on Mt Adams, I was unable to identify the myriad peaks that lay 'off the edge' of my particular map!

Finally, note that true left and true right in the route descriptions refer to the left or right bank respectively when going downstream with the flow of the river, creek or glacier.

HUTS AND HUT FEES

New Zealand's hut network includes over 1000 backcountry huts, a service second to none anywhere in the world. The huts do, however, require money for ongoing maintenance and periodic replacement, and it is vitally important that all hut users help out by paying for their overnight stays. All of the huts referred to in this book, with the exception of Mueller Hut at Aoraki/Mount Cook National Park, are covered by the DoC Annual Hut Pass. The pass is exceptionally good value for regular hut users, the initial cost being recovered after only six or seven hut bednights. By purchasing one of these passes at the start of the season, all further payment hassles can be forgotten for the next 12 months. Note that the pass is not valid for Great Walk huts.

Facilities in the backcountry huts vary from place to place and from hut to hut. Specific hut details have been included as they appear in the text, but remember that changes do happen. It is always a good idea to keep a finger on the backcountry's pulse

- - - - Track described	↟ Hut	\\ Falls	) (Tunnel
- - - - Route described	▸ Shelter/bivvy	⤜ Bridge	═ Wooden viaduct
—— 4 wheel drive track	⚐ Camp site	● Rock shelter/Cave	🛡63 State Highway
▲ Mountain	) (Saddle	⋐ Bluff	

by reading such publications as Wilderness Magazine and the Bulletin of the Federated Mountain Clubs.

HUT ETIQUETTE

At night or during bad weather, the hut forms the focus of the tramping experience and is part of the tradition of the New Zealand backcountry. A few simple courtesies make the experience an enjoyable one for all, even in a crowded hut.

Always make room for newcomers, even if the hut is nearing capacity. When the hut is full, consider using a tent if you have one. Inside, keep your gear tidy and contained, and try not to spread out too much. Remove wet boots before entering the hut to keep the floor clean and dry. Cook with ventilation, conserve firewood and don't overheat the hut to the discomfort of others. When leaving, make sure all benches and tables are clean, sweep the floor, close all windows and doors, and ensure you've put out the fire and replaced any firewood used. If you have spare room in your pack, consider taking out any extra rubbish left around, as it is surprising how huts can soon fill with 'forgotten' waste. You won't go far wrong if you follow the rule, 'Leave the hut as you'd hope to find it'.

CAMPING AND CONSERVATION

Over a third of the trips in this book have either camping as an option or, in several cases, as a necessity. The extra weight of a two-person flysheet, a small cooker and a foam mat is minimal when compared with the flexibility camping provides on any trip. However, always be careful when choosing a campsite: try to avoid camping under trees in stormy weather, or next to rising rivers or below loose bluffs in rain. Be aware of the fragile environment through which you are travelling: don't take away anything natural, and don't leave anything unnatural. Avoid lighting fires when they are unnecessary (in summer) or during a fire ban. When they are necessary, use pre-existing fireplaces and keep all fires small, as dead wood is a natural part of the ecology and in some places is in very short supply.

In the South Island we are blessed with some of the best water anywhere on this planet, but we need to work to keep it this way. Avoid polluting any waterways with soap or detergents, bury toilet waste well away from any water source (at least 100 metres if possible) and use permanent hut toilets whenever you can. In general, the rivers and streams encountered on these tramps are fine to drink from, but if in doubt boil or filter the water first.

SAFETY AND EQUIPMENT

There is not the scope in this book to give a detailed description of equipment and safety, but a brief list of what should be carried for a typical weekend tramp is as follows: sleeping bag, billy, burner, fuel, warm woolly hat, sunhat, gloves, raincoat, warm jersey or fleece, two pairs of polypropylene or woollen long-johns, two wool or polypropylene tops, a pair of shorts, first-aid kit, mug, plate, utensils, two pairs of warm socks, map, compass, sunscreen, candles, matches, and enough food for the trip's duration plus a few extra snacks and one extra meal. For some trips you will need to take a tent, or at least a flysheet and sleeping mat. In addition, some of the tramps described require the use of ice axes and crampons, particularly in winter or springtime.

You should leave your intentions, including possible bad-weather alternatives, with a trusted friend who can, in the event of your party becoming overdue, be relied upon to contact the Police Search and Rescue. Use DoC's 'sign in and sign out' system wherever possible.

Remember that rivers are the biggest hazard in the backcountry and cause the most deaths. You should be well versed in the current Mountain Safety Council river-crossing techniques, and have practised these before you need to use them in a real situation. Many tramping clubs offer introductory courses to river crossing, bushcraft and navigation.

Happy and safe tramping!

Barnett, S. *North Island Weekend Tramps* (Nelson: Craig Potton Publishing, 2002)

Barnett, S. & Brown, R. *Classic Tramping in New Zealand* (Nelson: Craig Potton Publishing, 1999)

Bishop, N. *Natural History of New Zealand* (Auckland: Hodder & Stoughton, 1992)

Brabyn, S. *Tramping in the South Island: Nelson Lakes to Arthurs Pass* (Christchurch: Brabyn Publishing, 1997)

Brabyn, S. & Bryant, E. *Tramping in the South Island: Arthurs Pass to Mt Cook* (Christchurch: Brabyn Publishing, 2001)

Crowe, A. *Which Native Tree?* (Auckland: Penguin, 1992)

Crowe, A. *Which Native Fern?* (Auckland: Penguin, 1994)

Crowe, A. *Which Native Forest Plant?* (Auckland: Penguin, 1994)

Dawson, J. & Lucas, R. *Nature Guide to the New Zealand Forest* (Auckland: Godwit, 2000)

McNeill, R. (ed.) *Moir's Guide South* (Christchurch: Great Lakes Southern Press, 1995)

Malcolm, B. & Malcolm, N. *New Zealand's Alpine Plants Inside and Out* (Nelson: Craig Potton Publishing, 1988)

Molloy, L. & Smith, R. *Landforms – The Shaping of New Zealand* (Nelson: Craig Potton Publishing, 2002)

Ombler, K. *National Parks and Other Wild Places of New Zealand* (Cape Town: Struik New Holland Publishers, 2001)

Pickering, M. & Smith, R. *101 Great Tramps in New Zealand* (Auckland: Reed, last revised 2001)

Pickering, M. *The Southern Journey* (Christchurch: privately published, 1993)

Potton, C. *Classic Walks of New Zealand* (Nelson: Craig Potton Publishing, 1997)

Salmon, J.T. *The Native Trees of New Zealand* (Auckland: Reed, 1980)

Spearpoint, G. *Waking to the Hills* (Auckland: Reed-Methuen, 1985)

Spearpoint, G. (ed.) *Moir's Guide North* (Lincoln, Canterbury: privately published, 1998)

Wilson, H. *Wild Plants of Mount Cook National Park* (Christchurch: Field Guide Publication, 1978)

Department of Conservation's National Park Handbooks are a mine of useful information.

NZ Wilderness is a monthly magazine that regularly features weekend tramps, as well as stories on conservation, exploration, mountain-biking, sea kayaking, climbing and natural history.

Bulletin of the Federated Mountain Clubs is published quarterly by the Federated Mountain Clubs of New Zealand (P.O. Box 1604, Wellington). It is free to members of affiliated clubs and contains topical issues and news items on the country's outdoors.

Upper Cobb Valley

Duration: 2 days.

Grade: Easy.

Time: 10 hours total. Trilobite Hut (at roadend; 12 bunks, wood stove) to Fenella Hut (12 bunks, wood stove, gas cooker): 5 hours.

Maps: Cobb M26, Mount Arthur M27, Kahurangi Parkmap 274/13.

Access: Along the Cobb Reservoir Road from SH 60 at Upper Takaka.

Alternative Routes: Ascents of Kakapo Peak or Mt Xenicus, given an extra day.

Information: DoC Motueka, Ph 03 528 9117; DoC Takaka, Ph 03 525 8444.

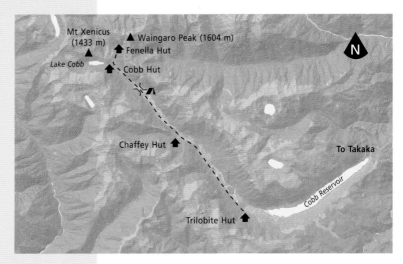

Kahurangi National Park is crisscrossed by an excellent range of tramping tracks. The walk up the Cobb Valley to a subalpine rock garden dotted with small tarns is one of the easier tramps, and apart from its relative remoteness from major centres (it is a 120-kilometre drive from Nelson) is a perfect introduction to the pleasures of weekend trips. It offers some easy tramping along a picturesque valley, followed by a short, steeper haul up to the well-known and very comfortable Fenella Hut.

The Cobb Valley is situated towards the northern end of Kahurangi National Park, and this trip involves a drive over Takaka Hill to the turn-off at Upper Takaka. The Cobb Reservoir Road winds its way from here for 37 rough kilometres (20 of them unsealed after the powerhouse), through the very scenic Takaka River Gorge, with occasional views southwards to the Mt Arthur Range (see next walk, page 15). The narrow road finally reaches the top end of the reservoir, where there are several good camping spots among the tussocks towards the water's edge. Alternatively, Trilobite Hut is well situated at the roadend for late arrivals (12 bunks and a wood stove).

The path from the Trilobite Hut along the classically glaciated Upper Cobb Valley passes through short sections of beech forest interspersed with extensive grassy flats. These meadows are covered with a rich array of alpine plants, in particular the yellow-headed Maori onion *(Bulbinella hookeri)*, which in high summer provides a riot of colour along the track. Unique to this area is the Cobb Valley gentian *(Gentiana* sp.), with its blue-mauve coloration – purple clusters of the flowers can be seen sprinkled across the landscape in the early summer. Also look out for various orchid species as you walk along: green-hooded, sun, mountain and the easy-to-identify odd-leaved orchid, which grows in profusion at selected shady spots along the way, are all reasonably common.

The historic but rather dilapidated Chaffey Hut (two bunks) is reached after two gentle hours. This beech-slab construction was built in the early 1950s by Jack McBurney, an early ranger in the Cobb, supposedly as a much-needed retreat from all the hustle and bustle associated with the dam construction down the valley. Nowadays, it provides an intimate shelter for two, away from possible crowds at the more distant Fenella Hut.

The old route crossed the river here, but a newly constructed track now carries along on the true right. Along the way, more sections of shady beech forest and grassy flats above the river are traversed before you pass the funky Tent Camp, a rustic alternative to the more permanent accommodation further up the valley. Side creeks are now bridged, making this an all-weather track, but be prepared for some fairly boggy sections during wet weather. The main river is crossed above Tent Camp, and the small but adequate Cobb Hut (four bunks), situated in a clearing among the twisted beech forest, is reached about two-and-a-half hours beyond Chaffey Hut.

The final half-hour to Fenella Hut climbs up through stunted, lichen-draped beech trees and passes alongside a narrow gorge where waterfalls cascade down its inaccessible depths. Fenella Hut (sleeps 12, wood stove and gas cooker) is set in an alpine rock garden of great variety at 1100 metres. It is a spacious and luxurious refuge, as well as an excellent base from which to explore the surrounding complex landscape. It was built in 1978, a year after Fenella Druce and her three companions were killed at Aoraki/Mount Cook National Park when the Three Johns Hut at Barron Saddle was

Fenella Hut, Cobb Valley

Towards Fenella Hut

blown off the mountain in a storm.

There are a number of interesting side trips possible from Fenella Hut, and an extra day would enable you to reach the top of either the 1783-metre Kakapo Peak, via Waingaro Peak, or the blocky summit of Xenicus Peak (1433 metres). Both of these worthwhile climbs offer some good exploring and more extensive views among the alpine rock gardens. Another popular side trip is to Lake Cobb and Round Lake, with the option of linking up with Mt Gibbs and Xenicus Peak. A more leisurely alternative is to amble the 'two furlongs' (or 400 metres in layman's terms) to a very picturesque swimming hole set among alpine vegetation and with fine views all around. This is just one of a number of small tarns that lie scattered around the low saddle between the Cobb and Burgoo valley systems.

Return to the roadend along the same track you followed in. There are some excellent swimming holes and diving rocks in the Takaka River shortly before you regain SH 60 – the perfect way to freshen up before the drive home.

Salisbury Tablelands/Mt Arthur

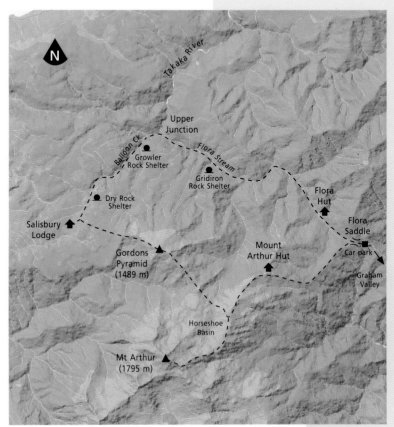

Duration: 2 days.

Grade: Moderate.

Time: 12 hours total. Graham Valley carpark to Salisbury Lodge (sleeps 24, gas cooker and heater): 4.5 hours. Salisbury Lodge to Graham Valley carpark via Mt Arthur: 8 hours.

Maps: Mount Arthur M27, Kahurangi Parkmap 274/13.

Access: From Motueka Valley Road, about 12 km south of Motueka township.

Information: DoC Motueka, Ph 03 528 9117.

WARNING! Limestone regions are often riddled with sinkholes, which can be obscured by thick bush or heavy snowfall.

This area is readily accessible from Nelson, and as the roadend is at almost 1000 metres it provides an easy start for trips in the Mt Arthur region. With a mixture of beech forests, subalpine tussock basins and bare limestone mountains, the Salisbury Tablelands and Mt Arthur area offers a wide variety of good tracks and huts. Trampers who come here are rewarded with sweeping views across the top of the Mainland and, on clear days, beyond Farewell Spit to Mt Taranaki. The route described offers the weekend tramper a taste of all the above, although good weather is recommended as there are some exposed mountaintop sections.

The Mt Arthur access road is signposted from a rickety-looking road bridge over the Motueka River, some 12 kilometres south of Motueka township and shortly before the settlement of Ngatimoti. The road up Graham Valley is steep and narrow, and not easily negotiable in wet or snowy conditions – be very careful of vehicles coming downhill. The carpark is at the respectable height of 920 metres, and has an information shelter, toilet and intentions book. From here, a broad 4WD locked road leads up to Flora Saddle. It is mostly downhill from the saddle to the junction with Balloon Creek, about two-and-a-half hours away.

The easy path sidles above the crystal waters of Flora Stream, a regular habitat for blue ducks (whio), which are most easily located by the telltale whistle of the male. This track was originally constructed by goldminers in the 1870s to access the Salisbury Tablelands; the latter was named after Thomas Salisbury, who grazed sheep on these upland grasslands to provide the diggers with fresh mutton.

The track passes an open clearing, where Flora Hut is sited (12 bunks and an open fireplace), and later on the massive limestone overhangs known as the Gridiron Rock Shelter, which no doubt proved a valuable bivvy for the itinerant goldminers who passed this way. A small four-bunk hut has been squeezed under the first of these, while the second one has room for eight on the wooden sleeping platforms. DoC has an ongoing pest-control programme based around these shelters as it attempts to create a 'mainland island' in the Flora Valley. Of primary concern is the continuing survival of the endangered *Powelliphanta* land snails, which live in these forests and are understandably a particular favourite for the many possums in the area. Beware of squashing these unique molluscs on the track, especially in wet weather.

En route to Mt Arthur, Kahurangi National Park

Tussock, Astelia sp. *and beech forest on the Salisbury Tablelands*

At the Upper Junction, Flora Stream flows on to meet the Takaka River, while the route up to the Salisbury Tablelands follows high above Balloon Creek through tall stands of red beech to the bushline, reached after about one-and-a-half hours. A further half-hour across tussock basins sees you at the well-positioned and spacious Salisbury Lodge (sleeps 24, gas cooker and heater), with grand views over to Mt Arthur and The Twins. In fine weather, alternative accommodation can be found at the Dry Rock Shelter, located up a small track at the bushline. This has a sleeping platform with foam mattresses that sleeps eight to 10, and looks out through a frame of beech trees and astelia fronds to the tussock basins beyond. Note that Hiking New Zealand, a commercial guiding company, uses this rock shelter on a weekly basis during summer, normally on Tuesday nights.

The route up the 1489-metre Gordons Pyramid starts some 500 metres back along the track you walked on day one. There is little or no water available for this long day's walk, as it traverses mostly porous limestone rock; in hot weather you should therefore ensure that you fill up your water bottles before you leave the hut.

The track crosses open tussock dotted with small tarns, before entering the dense forest of silver beech and, higher up, twisted and weatherbeaten rough-leaved tree daisies. The underlying topography is cloaked in the rich understorey of ferns and shrubs, and as this is a classic karst landscape care should be taken if you travel away from the path – potholes and bluffs most certainly lie in wait for the unwary. The track climbs steeply to the bushline, marked with a large red shield. From here, a poled route leads steadily uphill, passing a large rock outcrop, to the top of Gordons Pyramid, reached about two hours after leaving the hut.

Should poor weather prevent a full traverse of the tops, an escape route exists from the third marker on the climb up to Gordons Pyramid. From this point, contour round to Cloustons Mine at the bush edge, from where a good track zigzags down to Flora Stream.

Fine panoramas are to be had from the summit of Gordons Pyramid, with the rolling Salisbury Tablelands stretched out below, densely forested valleys leading westwards to Karamea and the thin line of Farewell Spit visible between the foreground hills. These views continue as the route now follows the broad grassy ridgeline to the southeast, passing a small, signposted tarn that provides the only water until the well-positioned Mount Arthur Hut is reached (eight bunks, gas heater but no cooker).

The route along this undulating ridge is poled throughout, eventually dropping down into the bare marble bowl known as Horseshoe Basin. Sinkholes abound here, often providing a sheltered haven for many of the unique alpine species that flourish in Northwest Nelson. Particularly showy are the large yellow mountain buttercups, or korikori, which flower in springtime. While wandering across this karst landscape it is also worth appreciating that New Zealand's deepest cave system lies somewhere beneath your feet. The 889-metre-deep, 23-kilometre-long Nettlebed Cave offers a challenging two- to three-day adventure for experienced cavers.

The route out of Horseshoe Basin climbs up to the ridge running northeast from Mt Arthur. An ascent of the 1795-metre-high Mt Arthur itself requires an additional two hours and should only be climbed in good weather as the ridge is exposed to winds from most directions. A well-worn path leads up, via some easy scrambling and a short section of loose scree, to the flat-topped summit, with its fine views in all directions. The peaks known as The Twins, three kilometres to the southwest, are a mere 15 metres higher than Mt Arthur itself.

Alternatively, after climbing out of Horseshoe Basin continue northwards to Mount Arthur Hut at the bushline. From here a broad, easy track through beautiful stands of mountain neinei leads back down to Flora Saddle and the carpark.

Mt Owen

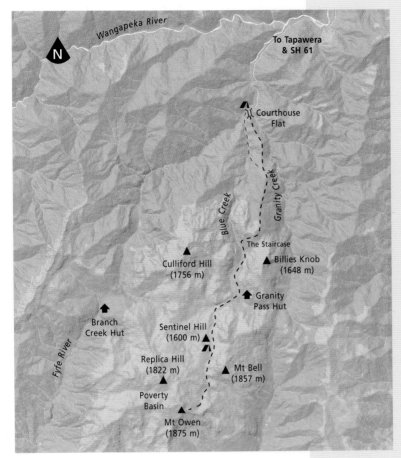

Duration: 2–3 days.

Grade: Moderate.

Time: 14–15 hours total. Courthouse Flat to Granity Pass Hut (6 bunks, wood stove): 5 hours. Granity Pass Hut to Mt Owen: 3 hours. Mt Owen to Courthouse Flat: 6–7 hours.

Map: Wangapeka M28.

Access: SH 61, along the Motueka River Valley. Turn off at Tapawera for Wangapeka Track.

Alternative Routes: Fyfe River Valley on the descent (pick-up required).

Information: DoC Motueka, Ph 03 528 9117; DoC St. Arnaud, Ph 03 521 1806.

WARNING! The terrain is often rough and peppered with sinkholes and rocky clefts, which present hidden hazards after heavy snowfall.

Mt Owen is one of those special places in Kahurangi National Park and deserves a three-day weekend in order to explore fully the various nooks and crannies this complex massif has to offer. It is the marble mountain par excellence, possessing many of the unique aspects the region of Northwest Nelson has, until relatively recently, kept largely to itself. The original Ordovician limestone here, which formed 500 million years ago, has been metamorphosed through intense pressure and temperature into a recrystallised marble. More recently, icecaps smothered these marble uplands, their radiating glaciers putting the finishing touches on what is today considered a fairly unusual landscape.

At 1875 metres Mt Owen is the highest peak in the area, with views to match its lofty status across some very undeveloped and suitably rugged landscapes. The mountain can be approached both from the north and south, but here only the northern approach, via Granity Pass Hut, is described. The routes up from the south – either via Sunrise Peak, Bulmer Creek or the Fyfe River – are all rewarding trips, although harder and longer. As the only hut along the route has just six bunks, it is a good idea to carry a tent. This also gives you the flexibility of camping away from the main trail, although water is scarce across this limestone region.

Mt Owen, Kahurangi National Park

The track starts at Courthouse Flat, which is situated at the end of the 32-kilometre road from Tapawera. This road winds alongside the Wangapeka River and is mostly narrow and unsealed, with a few concrete fords (crossing these should present no problem except during or just after heavy rain). There is a campsite and a DoC information kiosk with an intentions book and telephone about four kilometres before the end of the road, plus a small four-bunk hut a kilometre further on at Rolling Junction (the start of the Wangapeka Track).

Courthouse Flat is another three kilometres from Rolling Junction and has ample space for camping, with a toilet and water from the creek. Its name is derived from its goldmining past, which saw a small settlement spring up here, complete with a jail and courthouse. As was often the case, expectations exceeded the economic reality and nature is once more taking over.

There are initially two options for the approach to Mt Owen, both by way of the Billies Knob Track. One follows the steep ridge between Blue and Granity creeks, while the other follows Blue Creek before ascending steeply for 450 metres to the ridge where both tracks meet. The latter is a shadier option on a hot day, although the ridge route is more straightforward. In either case, take plenty of water as you pass only one intermittent stream in the entire five or so hours to the hut.

The track along Blue Creek passes a collection of long-abandoned goldmining relics, which no doubt resulted in the financial ruin of many an investor in the late 1800s, while the ridge track climbs steadily through manuka and broadleaf scrub, offering glimpses over the Granity Creek Gorge. Both tracks meet after an hour and a half where a more shady, mature beech forest takes over. The route then continues uphill for a further hour at a slightly more gentle pace to a burnt clearing above the bushline – a good lunch spot. There are views to the north and west from here, across to the monolithic Mt Patriarch and the closer Culliford Hill.

Poles now lead across open tussock and back into the forest to Billies Saddle, from where a steep descent through imposing limestone bluffs (known as The Staircase) leads to the upper section of Blue Creek, at this point usually waterless. There is often a small stream trickling across the track below the bluffs, which is the only water encountered en route to the hut.

The track now stays down in the valley, passing a prospector's slab hut (now derelict) and continuing along boulders up the dry Blue Creek. The forest along this section is wonderfully varied, with mountain neinei dominating the scene, its unusual candelabra shape and 'pineapple' flowerheads being easily recognisable. Also along the track are fine examples of the rough-leaved tree daisy and some particularly impressive speargrasses that should be given a wide berth. This rich array of subalpine vegetation contrasts with bare rocky crags rising steeply overhead.

Granity Pass Hut is situated at the entrance to Ghost Valley, on a small hebe-covered terrace on the true right of the creek. This is a standard six-bunk hut with a pot-bellied stove, although as firewood is limited in the subalpine zone be sure to bring a cooker with you. Camping is possible near the hut, although a better spot is located a further hour or so around Sentinel Hill, at a cluster of small tarns directly below Mt Owen.

Mt Owen, the highest peak in Kahurangi National Park at 1875 metres, can be reached from the Granity Pass Hut in about three hours. It would, however, be a pity to hurry through this remarkable landscape, so it is well worth giving yourself an extra day or two to explore fully the various ridges and basins and the bizarrely sculptured

Mt Owen reflected in a tarn

limestone outcrops that abound across this plateau.

From the hut, a well-defined track heads up through Ghost Valley along the crest of an old glacial moraine, known as the Railway Embankment. This is a reminder that ice was a major influence in the creation of this landscape, subsequently modified to a lesser degree by water and wind. Tussocklands lead around the eastern side of Sentinel Hill to a cluster of tarns occupying a shallow, marshy basin; these contain the last water for the day unless patches of winter snow linger on the tops.

Above these tarns, the cairned track weaves through a fascinating array of rough marble formations, water-worn flutings, vertical-sided crevasses and weird rock towers. During the summer months a remarkable variety of alpine flowers seek shelter among the rock outcrops: the showy yellow buttercup (korikori), a number of daisy species, ourisias, short and tall gentians, euphrasias, bright yellow bulbinellas, anisotomes, epilobiums, hebes and cushion plants, to name but a few. More than 60 alpine plant species are found exclusively in Northwest Nelson, due to the region having escaped the worst of the destructive glaciation that wiped out many species further south between 10,000 and 20,000 years ago.

The summit of Mt Owen is adorned with a collection of old survey posts and concrete bases, although they fail to detract from the spectacular panorama stretched out below in all directions. A worthwhile side trip from here drops down the southern aspect of the mountain. Carefully weave your way through the chaotic rock garden below to reach a prominent bare-rock knob overlooking the Bulmer Valley. This valley provides access to New Zealand's longest cave network, the Bulmer System, which extends under Mt Owen for about 40 kilometres and is the domain of serious speleologists.

From this rock garden it is then possible to reach Castle Basin and cross an obvious saddle into Poverty Basin – tarns occupy both of these depressions. Various routes lead from here, either back to the summit plateau or around the massif to regain the track at the Sentinel Hill tarns.

An alternative escape route leads northwest from Poverty Basin by skirting Replica Hill to Pt 1500 and down through forest to the six-bed Branch Creek Hut, situated towards the headwaters of the Fyfe River. The track down to the Owen River along this valley is straightforward but long (allow six to seven hours), and unless transport arrangements have been made it will leave you stranded up a quiet side road some considerable distance from the Wangapeka Valley.

Otherwise, return from the Mt Owen summit the way you came, taking the alternative Blue Creek or ridge track and enjoying a dip in Nuggety Creek to end the day.

Thousand Acre Plateau

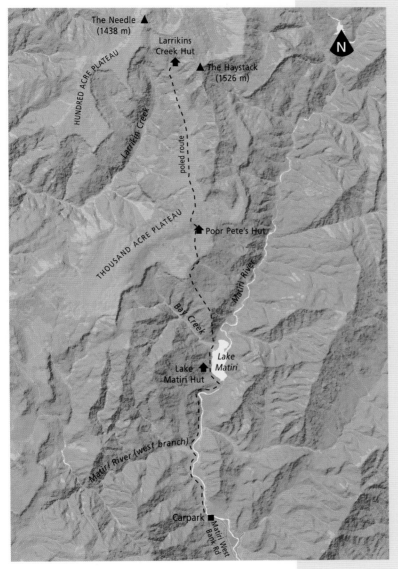

The Needle ▲
(1438 m)

Larrikins
Creek Hut ▲

▲ The Haystack
(1526 m)

HUNDRED ACRE PLATEAU

Larrikin Creek

poled route

THOUSAND ACRE PLATEAU

▲ Poor Pete's Hut

Matiri River

Bay Creek

Lake
Matiri

Lake ▲
Matiri Hut

Matiri River (west branch)

Carpark ■

Matiri West
Bank Rd

N

Duration: 2 days.

Grade: Moderate.

Time: 10 hours total, excluding side trip. Matiri Valley Road end to Poor Pete's Hut (3 bunks): 6 hours. Side trip from Poor Pete's Hut to Larrikins Creek Hut (6 bunks): 3 hours. Poor Pete's Hut to Matiri Valley Road end: 4 hours.

Maps: Murchison M29, Wangapeka M28, Kahurangi Parkmap 274/13.

Access: From SH 6, 6 km north of Murchison, turn onto the Matiri Valley Road.

Alternative Routes: Continue to Larrikins Hut and climb the Needle and Haystack.

Information: Murchison Visitor Information Centre, Ph 03 523 9350.

The Thousand Acre Plateau and nearby Hundred Acre Plateau represent classic limestone land-forms that appear fairly impregnable from afar, but in the case of the former can be visited in a weekend. For those who make the effort, the 700-metre climb from the valley floor to the almost horizontal tablelands at the 1100-metre contour will be a

Thousand Acre Plateau

memorable excursion into one of the many unusual landscapes of Kahurangi National
Park. The rolling tussock- and herb-covered tops of the Thousand Acre Plateau are
guarded by an impressive escarpment of steep limestone bluffs, giving this isolated
upland area a 'Lost World' feel. The plateaux survive because a thick, hard limestone
cap overlays the softer sandstone sediments below; the gentler slopes beneath this ero-
sion-resistant rim are today largely covered by forest. These upland areas form part of
the catchment for the Matiri River, which in turn flows into the mighty Buller.

The Matiri Valley Road branches off from the main highway six kilometres north
of Murchison township. A 20-minute drive through farmland leads to the end of the
public road, where a carpark, DoC sign and intentions book mark the start of the 4WD
track up the valley.

A gentle hour through farm paddocks leads to the west branch of the Matiri River.
It is possible to boulder-hop across this in low flow, but it is unbridged and the going
can become difficult and dangerous after heavy rain. On the far bank, by the edge of
the forest, there is an old, characterful beech-slab hut, nowadays derelict. Beyond this,
the old pack track sidles easily above the main river, reaching the well-placed Lake
Matiri Hut (six bunks) after another hour. This hut commands a fine view over the lake
and up the valley, and is a good spot for a rest before the climbing begins.

The track contours above the western shore of the lake, often home to a number
of paradise shelducks, before dropping down to cross the outwash fan of Bay Creek

(there are good campsites and swimming nearby). The 700-metre climb onto the plateau starts just after Bay Creek flats, and is well marked throughout. Climb steadily through stands of hard and silver beech to a cleared viewpoint overlooking the valley and Lake Matiri, now far below.

The forest types are quite diverse along this track, from various beech species to rata, kamahi and mountain cedar, as well as podocarps such as rimu and mountain toatoa. The track relents a little as it passes through mountain neinei and bushes of rough-leaved tree daisy, before weaving among large, chaotic limestone blocks near the top of the upper escarpment.

At the plateau rim, the forest abruptly gives way to open tussocklands, across which a poled route leads, after half an hour, to the dilapidated Poor Pete's Hut (three bunks). Although the hut makes a suitable shelter from a storm, nearby are preferable campsites where you can enjoy the open expanses of the Thousand Acre Plateau in the evening.

If time is limited to a weekend, then the morning of the second day would be best spent exploring the area in the vicinity of Poor Pete's Hut. From Pt 1167 (the high point about three kilometres southwest from the hut) there are great views across to the Hundred Acre Plateau and Mt Misery, The Needle and The Haystack. In summer, the plateau comes alive with a profusion of large white and orange daisies *(Celmisia monroi)*, a welcome contrast to the muted browns and

Lake Matiri near Murchison, Kahurangi National Park

greens that make up the landscape for much of the year. Given time, a trip to Larrikins Creek Hut (six bunks) and a visit to the Hundred Acre Plateau, combined with an ascent of The Needle, would give a better overview of the complex topography that makes up these unique limestone plateaux.

Mt Stokes

Duration: 1 day.

Grade: Moderate.

Time: 5–6 hours.

Maps: Cape Jackson Q26, Marlborough Sounds 336/07.

Access: Kenepuru Road onto Titirangi Road; start walk at junction of Titirangi Road and Anakoha Road.

Information: DoC Picton, Ph 03 520 3007.

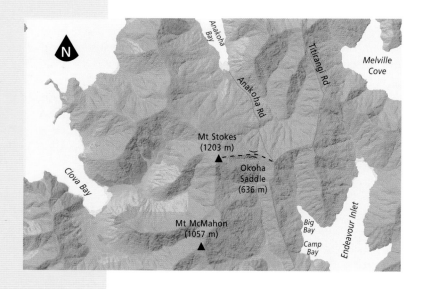

Mt Stokes is the highest point in the Marlborough Sounds, commanding excellent vistas over the top of the South Island and across to the bottom of the North Island. Starting at about 550 metres above sea level, the climb to the Mt Stokes summit (1203 m) is mostly along a track through mixed forest types – the open tops are reached only in the last half-hour.

Drive up along Titirangi Road to its junction with Anakoha Road. Vehicles can be left at this saddle, where there is a DoC sign marking the start of the track. Initially, the trail is quite rough underfoot, with the usual blend of tree roots, rocks and mud to contend with, although it is always well marked with the ubiquitous orange triangles. The forest type here is predominantly beech, with some particularly fine stands of red beech and a rich understorey of mosses and ferns. The track through the forest skirts the northern slopes of Mt Robinson, levelling out after half an hour as it crosses Ohoka Saddle.

It is a steep climb from here to the bushline, gaining some 500 metres of elevation in barely 1.5 kilometres. Shortly below the bushline, the beech forest starts to thin out before abruptly emerging onto a rocky knoll and tussocky tops.

The Inland Kaikouras from Mt Stokes, with Picton below

The actual summit of Mt Stokes is a further 15 minutes away along these tops, with the approaching cluster of radio and telecommunication towers that litter the highest point in the Marlborough Sounds failing to detract from the all-encompassing views to be had.

Spread out in all directions is a bewildering array of narrow inlets, sweeping bays and sinuous, bush-clad headlands that typify the drowned river valley topography of this area. Directly below is Endeavour Inlet, along the shores of which the Queen Charlotte Track wends its way from Ship Cove to Anakiwa (see following walk). To the east, the hazy shape of the Kapiti Coast, at the bottom of the North Island, is strung out on the horizon, while the southern vista is dominated by the bulk of the Inland Kaikouras. Mt Tapuae-o-Uenuku and Alarm are clearly visible beyond Picton, over 100 kilometres away.

The descent to the road is by the same route, and is, of course, somewhat faster than the ascent.

Endeavour Inlet from Mt Stokes

Queen Charlotte Walkway

MARLBOROUGH SOUNDS

Duration: 3–5 days.

Grade: Moderate.

Time: 25 hours total. Ship Cove to Camp Bay: 9 hours. Camp Bay to Portage: 8 hours. Portage to Anakiwa: 8 hours.

Maps: Cape Jackson Q26, Picton P27, Cook Strait Q27, Marlborough Sounds 336/07.

Access: Water taxi from Picton to Ship Cove, or depart from Anakiwa, off Queen Charlotte Drive.

Information: DoC Picton, Ph 03 520 3007.

WARNING! There is a total fire ban along the track, so bring your own cooker if you plan to camp.

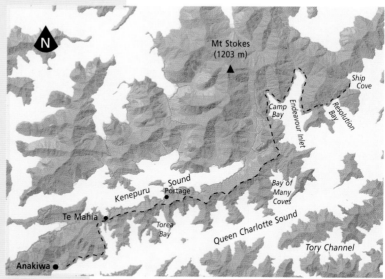

The Queen Charlotte Track differs from all the other walks in this book in so far as it passes through areas of permanent settlement, crosses roads and can be entered or exited at a number of places en route, either by car or boat. The entire track also takes longer than a weekend – between three and five days is recommended. It traverses a spectacular section of the Marlborough Sounds, from historic Ship Cove (boat access only) to the road at Anakiwa, passing through dense coastal forest, around bays and headlands, and along the ridgetop that forms the backbone of the finger of land rising between Kenepuru and Queen Charlotte sounds.

The track is good throughout, being wide and benched in many places, but there are some stiff climbs and it can be muddy and slippery in the wet. A reasonable level of fitness is therefore required to complete the whole 67-kilometre route. However, because of the track's ease of access, you can walk just some sections, taking a water taxi for others, and you can have your pack transported by boat operators to your evening's destination. Mountain biking is also permitted on the track, except along the section from Ship Cove to Kenepuru Saddle between 1 December and 28 February. Walkers have right of way over mountain-bikers.

The track can be walked in either direction, but is normally started at Ship Cove as the commercial boats from Picton operate in this direction. The description below is divided into three days, giving roughly eight hours' walking each day, although this can easily be extended to five days as accommodation is available at regular intervals.

Endeavour Inlet, Marlborough Sounds

Ship Cove, as it is now known, was a popular anchorage for Captain Cook during his three voyages to New Zealand in the 1770s. In fact, the sheltered harbour and abundant food supply kept him and his crew here for a total of 100 days over a seven-year spell. A morning boat service from Picton will get you to Ship Cove by 11.30am, and as camping is not allowed here it is necessary to start walking the day of arrival.

The track climbs away from the cove through thick, shady forest to a lookout, from where the inner and outer sounds are visible. The track then drops back down near the coast at Resolution Bay, reached after two hours. Continue over a small ridge and into the deep bay of Endeavour Inlet via an old bridle path, which sidles down to the shoreline and up to the head of the inlet, three hours from Resolution Bay. Antimony, used for hardening lead and pewter, was mined here in the 1880s and a small town sprang up to cater to the miners' needs. Nowadays, holiday homes, cabins and luxury lodges dot the forested hillsides above the inlet.

Follow the western shore of Endeavour Inlet through regrowth forest to Camp Bay, four hours beyond. A DoC campsite and lodge/hostel accommodation can be found here.

It is advisable to carry water between the Kenepuru and Te Mahia saddles; although the DoC campsites at the Bay of Many Coves and Black Rock have supplies of water, it apparently requires boiling. This section between Camp Bay and Portage is the longest and most strenuous of the trip, unless your journey is broken at either of the campsites en route.

Climb back up to Kenepuru Saddle and rejoin the track as it follows the crest of the ridge between the two sounds below; there are some fine vistas along this part of the trail. Two DoC campsites are passed along this ridge (Bay of Many Coves, three hours from Camp Bay, and Black Rock Camp, both with water, toilets and cooking shelters), before you eventually drop down to Torea Saddle and the road, four to five hours from the Bay of Many Coves. Turn right and walk down the road for 15 minutes to Portage, where a shop, hotel and DoC campsite at nearby Cowshed Bay are to be found.

Starting back up at Torea Saddle, the route continues on the exposed ridgetop, passing through plenty of gorse and manuka scrub. Be on the lookout here in spring-time for the small, unobtrusive green hooded orchids (*Pterostylis* sp.) that grow abundantly alongside the track.

At Te Mahia Saddle turn left for the secluded Mistletoe Bay, reached after four hours. There is a good DoC campsite here, plus three lodges that can be pre-booked through DoC at Picton. Alternatively, head to the right and down to reach Te Mahia resort, where a store and full range of accommodation are to be found.

The final four hours or so of the Queen Charlotte Track continue along an old bridle path high above the head of the sound before descending to Umungata (Davies Bay), location of the last (or first) campsite on the track. Note that camping is not permitted at the trailhead by Anakiwa, which is reached after a 45-minute stroll through mature beech forest along the shore. There is a shelter, toilets, a public phone and a carpark here. Public transport (bus or boat) is available from Anakiwa. The Outward Bound jetty is private – please use the Tirimoana Jetty, 800 metres further on.

Endeavour Inlet from Mt Stokes

MOUNT RICHMOND FOREST PARK

Mt Richmond

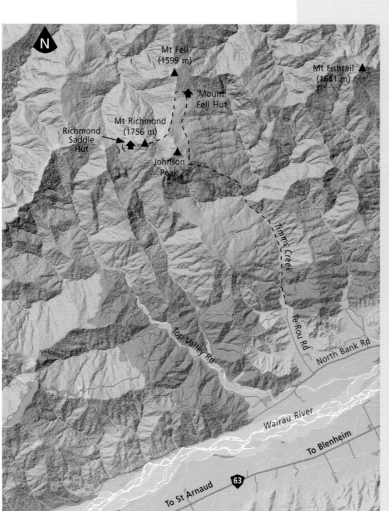

Duration: 2 days.

Grade: Moderate.

Time: 12–14 hours total. Timms Valley Road carpark to Mount Fell Hut (6 bunks, wood stove): 5–6 hours. Mount Fell Hut to Mt Richmond summit: 2–3 hours. Mt Richmond to Jubilee Flat: 5 hours.

Maps: Wairau 028, Mount Richmond State Forest Parkmap 274/06.

Access: Follow SH 6 for 16 km out of Blenheim to just beyond the bridge over the Wairau River at Renwick. Turn west here along North Bank Road to reach Te Rou Road after 30 km. The 3-km unsealed Timms Valley Road leads to a carpark and the start of the track.

Alternative Routes: A round trip can be undertaken from Timms Valley to Top Valley Road, although logging in Top Valley may restrict access from time to time.

Information: DoC Renwick, Ph 03 572 9100. For information on the current logging situation in Top Valley, contact Weyerhaeuser NZ Inc, Ph 03 543 8115.

Warning! Logging trucks use North Bank Road and the side roads off it, and there is also limited access to the area when logging is in progress – phone for information in advance (see above).

The Mount Richmond Forest Park is a surprisingly neglected tract of forest-clad mountains with isolated tussock and rock-strewn tops. It is sometimes referred to as the 'only part of the North Island in the South Island', as the rolling tops and bush-cloaked valleys have a distinctly North Island feel to them. The unique aspect of this area is further reinforced by the presence of the North Island edelweiss *(Leucogenes leontopodium)* and other species of alpine flora endemic to these ranges.

The whole forest park is very well serviced by good huts and a well-maintained track system, and offers a variety of tramps from day trips to the so-called 'Alpine Route', which takes four to five days to complete. The tramp described here is easily achievable in a weekend, and includes an ascent of the park's second-highest peak, Mt Richmond, at 1756 metres.

The track starts from the carpark at the end of Te Rou Road, heading along Timms Creek and up to Mount Fell Hut, an ascent of 1000 metres over about six hours. The initial section of Timms Valley consists of exotic plantations that are periodically being logged, so the track may be rather messy to begin with. It is, however, well signposted, so persevere for 45 minutes to reach the native bush and the official forest park boundary.

From here on, the forest is a varied mixture of beech trees, along with some fine stands of old podocarp species that thrive on the wetter, southern slopes of these ranges. All of the 'famous five' podocarps (miro, matai, rimu, totara and kahikatea) can be found along the way, with some particularly magnificent specimens of matai displaying the characteristic hammered-bark appearance on their straight, thick trunks.

The track follows the true right bank of the creek, crossing an open grassy clearing at Timms Flat before plunging back into the forest. Timms Creek is a delightfully clear, emerald-green as it tumbles over smooth river rocks; you pass a very inviting swimming hole along the way, worth sampling on a hot day. The track crosses a few minor side creeks, and then after

The Inland Kaikouras from Mt Richmond

two hours a larger creek with a small waterfall is reached. This marks the start of the uphill climb to the bushline hut and is the last water before you reach the hut in a further four hours.

The track is quite steep but well marked as it heads up a forested spur consisting largely of red and mountain beech, along with isolated specimens of totara. The forest floor is covered with a rich carpet of *Blechnum* fern species, in particular the resilient crown fern, or piupiu. The bushline at this relatively northern latitude extends beyond the 1300 metre contour on many slopes, and the track commences its long sidle to the hut at about this level after some three hours of steady uphill travel.

A more direct approach to Mt Richmond can be made from this point by heading directly to the tussock tops a short distance above, then traversing Johnson Peak and joining the poled route to the summit. However, to follow our route to Mount Fell Hut (six bunks plus wood stove), you skirt just below the bush edge for a further hour. The views are somewhat limited from the hut, as it is set among the stunted beech forest, but a short evening stroll onto the open tops will reward you with excellent panoramas in every direction.

There are a number of options for the next day, or two if time allows. A whole day could be spent exploring the open tops, climbing Mt Richmond and Mt Fell, and traversing these gentle ridges, taking in the views and enjoying botanical pursuits. If you are making the ascent of Mt Richmond, it is worth getting an early start – the open tops are only a couple of hundred metres above the hut, so there is a good chance you will enjoy a spectacular sunrise and be on the summit before the day has grown old.

A track leads up from the hut to a broad saddle overlooking Tasman Bay and Kahurangi National Park, where a small tarn and sign show the way to nearby Mt Fell. Poles lead south from this saddle, bypassing Pt 1613 on its eastern side and continuing towards the rocky pyramid of Mt Richmond. A second saddle is then crossed, where the daisy *Celmisia macmahonii*, endemic only to this park, grows in sizeable clusters between the tussocks. Later in the season, creamy-white gentians hide among the grasses here.

The final 250 metres up the east ridge consists of a jumble of boulders and small patches of scree, through which a good trail winds directly to the rocky summit of Mt Richmond. Along the way, be on the lookout for some large clumps of the so-called vegetable sheep, *Raoulia eximia*. These plants are superbly adapted and highly specialised members of the daisy family, with stems squeezed together so closely that the plant has an external cushion-like appearance, presenting a tightly packed mat that protects it from both summer drought and the icy winter winds common at these altitudes.

Tramper en route to Mt Richmond

At 1756 metres, Mt Richmond is surpassed in this range only by Red Hill, much further west, which is all of 34 metres higher. Nevertheless, the views from the Mount Richmond Forest Park's second-highest peak are second to none, with outstanding panoramas across to Mts Arthur and Owen in the west, Tapuae-o-Uenuku and neighbouring peaks of the Inland Kaikouras to the east, and the peaks of the Nelson Lakes National Park in the southwest. Far to the north, beyond the intervening ridges of the Marlborough Sounds ranges, lie the Tararuas of the North Island, with the distinctive cone of Mt Taranaki visible on a clear day suspended above the northern horizon. Closer at hand, Mt Fishtail presents a craggy aspect to the east, while other ridges and tops north of the long and straight Wairau Valley lie waiting to be explored.

The snow-covered peaks of Kahurangi National Park from Mt Richmond

A track leads from this summit to Richmond Saddle, an hour below, and an eight-berth hut, from where a steady descent down a forested spur leads to Top Valley and its roadend. This descent takes about five hours from the summit to Jubilee Flat; the Te Rou Road carpark is a further 12 km from here along the road.

If a pre-placed car or mountain bike has been left at the Top Valley roadend, then this round trip is quite feasible. However, if you choose to return along your route in, back down the valley from Mount Fell Hut, then you will be able to enjoy a pleasant morning on the tops – including the ascent of Mt Richmond – unencumbered by a heavy pack. It is always surprising how the same track can appear so different when approached from the other direction, providing the ideal opportunity to observe details in the forest that were missed on the way in.

Lake Angelus

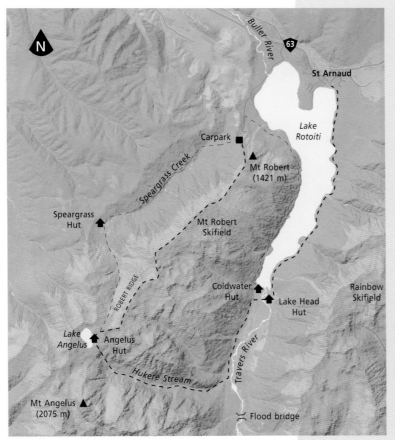

Duration: 2 days.

Grade: Moderate.

Time: 11–14 hours total. Mt Robert carpark to Angelus Hut (40 bunks, stove) via Robert Ridge: 6–7 hours. Angelus Hut to Coldwater Hut (6 bunks, wood stove) or Lake Head Hut (35 bunks, wood stove): 3–4 hours. Lake Head Hut to St Arnaud: 2–3 hours.

Maps: St Arnaud N29, Murchison M29, Nelson Lakes Parkmap 273/05.

Access: Take the West Bay Road from SH 63, about 2 km west of St Arnaud, and follow this via a series of switchbacks to the Mt Robert carpark.

Alternative Routes: An alternative exit is via Speargrass Creek. Summer side trip to Mt Angelus, via Sunset Saddle. Water taxis are available to the jetty by Coldwater Hut.

Information: DoC St Arnaud, Ph 03 521 1806.

WARNING! The route climbs to 1800 m in this alpine area and is very exposed to sudden changes of weather. Particular care is required if snow is lying on the ridgetops, when ice axe and crampons may be necessary.

A trip up to the alpine tarn of Lake Angelus, nestled in a glacial basin high above Lakes Rotoroa and Rotoiti, is one of the classic tramps in the Nelson Lakes National Park. This lake, at 1600 metres above sea level, can be reached by a number of routes, some more exposed to the elements than others. The Robert Ridge route is the most popular approach to the lake, and justifiably so, but should only be tackled in good weather as the ridge is very exposed for several hours along its length, with no easy escape route if conditions turn nasty. The lake and nearby spacious hut can be visited in an ordinary weekend, although an extra day spent among the rocky tops of the range – possibly including a scramble up Mt Angelus – would be a memorable addition to this tramp.

The high-altitude start at Mt Robert carpark (880 metres), if reached by car, will be appreciated as you zigzag steeply up the Pinchgut Track to a bushline shelter and the 1421-metre-high Mt Robert just above. Any weariness you experience from the climb should drop away as the stunning views unfold all around: down to the left and right, where both Lakes Rotoroa and Rotoiti lie cradled in their forested basins, and across a seemingly endless array of ridges and summits stretching in every direction. Allow one-and-a-half to two hours to reach the rounded top of this peak.

Once this sharp climb is behind you, you can enjoy the gently undulating ridge that leads off to the south. This is the route to Lake Angelus, and although it climbs to over 1800 metres it is nowhere near as steep as the initial haul up from the road. The route passes above basins to the east, where buildings and lift lines belonging to the Mt Robert Ski Club can be spotted on what is one of the oldest club fields in the country. In good visibility this open tops travel should present no difficulty, as the track is well worn by countless pairs of boots and frequent poles guide the way.

Various high points are encountered along the increasingly shattered ridge. First, you come to Flagtop (1690 metres), then you carry on down to a saddle just north of Julius Summit. At 1794 metres, this craggy peak is normally bypassed to the west, but in snowy or icy conditions it is usually safer to remain on the crest of the ridge rather than to attempt a potentially risky traverse. Some three to four hours after leaving the

Angelus Hut, Nelson Lakes National Park

Beech forest reflected in Lake Rotoiti

bushline the ridge drops a little. The track skirts scree slopes where necessary to avoid sharper sections above, before reaching a broad saddle between Speargrass Creek and a view down into the Angelus Basin.

Speargrass Creek provides an alternative exit back to the valley if necessary. There is a six-bunk hut at Speargrass Flat, reached after a three-hour descent, and from here it is a further two hours to the Mt Robert carpark. This valley is considerably more sheltered than the ridge above and is the recommended bad-weather escape from Angelus Hut, especially during the winter months when the upper reaches of Hukere Stream may be covered with snow and ice.

The idyllic Lake Angelus and its palatial hut now lie directly below, with only 15 minutes scrambling down a rocky ridge and an easy few minutes across tussock flats to the hut. Pause awhile before you start your descent to study the map and work out possible routes for the following day's exploration around this barren yet very attractive alpine basin.

Angelus Hut has room for up to 40 trampers, with a stove (coal usually provided) but no cooking facilities. Be prepared for plenty of international company over the summer months, as this is a popular place for overseas visitors as well as New Zealanders. Camping is actively discouraged around the fragile lakeshore, but nearby Hinapouri Tarn provides a quieter alternative for those who are prepared to carry camping gear along Robert Ridge.

An extra day spent wandering around this alpine basin should be included if at all possible. In summer, the 2075-metre Mt Angelus can be climbed without any special equipment from Sunset Saddle, offering spectacular views across Nelson Lakes

National Park. Alternatively, the whole day could just as easily be spent on the hut balcony with a good book, or indulging in some alpine botany among the rocks and tussocks that fringe the lake.

There is a contrasting and interesting return route from the Angelus Basin to the Travers Valley and back to St Arnaud via the verdant Hukere Stream. The track from the lakeshore drops steeply through bluffs and scree slopes into the headwaters of the Hukere Stream; care should be taken here, as slippery tussocks and small waterslides have to be negotiated. The track through this rough alpine basin is well marked with cairns and poles, and soon enters beech forest that grows alongside the tumbling stream. The Cascade Track, which follows the true right of this stream, is a visual delight, with every subtle shade of green represented along the way. It weaves steeply downhill between mossy boulders and lichen-draped mountain beech trees, very typical of the forest type encountered in the Nelson Lakes area.

There is a drop of 1000 metres from Lake Angelus to the Travers River, and after two to three knee-punishing hours of descent the final hour of gentle valley travel to either Coldwater Hut (six bunks, wood stove in the porch) or Lake Head Hut (35 bunks and wood stove) is a most welcome change. There is a good track along the true left side of this broad valley, and the Travers River can usually be crossed when you are almost opposite Lake Head Hut if you are heading back by this route. Should the river be running high, use the swingbridge half an hour up the main river from the Hukere Stream confluence, or remain on the western shores all the way out.

If you are picking up a vehicle at the Mt Robert carpark, the Lakeside Track, which follows the western side of Lake Rotoiti, is a better option although it is slightly longer. From Coldwater Hut, amble through mature stands of red, silver and black beech, along with isolated rata and kamahi, to join the Mt Robert Road after about three hours. A final uphill stretch along the road leads to the carpark and the start point of the trip.

Alternatively, follow the east side of the lake, starting at the larger Lake Head Hut and entering the Rotoiti mainland island conservation area as the village of St Arnaud is approached. The concept of a mainland 'island' is to eradicate all pests within a controlled area, usually with definite physical boundaries across which reinfestation is unlikely. The success of this project, and many others like it around the country, will become apparent when the all-too-silent forests of New Zealand once again echo to the sound of birdcalls.

Mole Tops

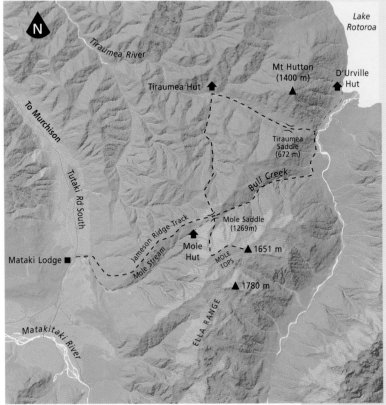

Lake Rotoroa

Duration: 2–3 days.

Grade: Moderate.

Time: 16–17 hours total. Mataki Lodge to Mole Hut (4 bunks) or Mole Saddle: 3 hours. Mole Saddle to Tiraumea Hut (6 bunks): 3–4 hours. Tiraumea Hut to D'Urville River: 2 hours. D'Urville River to Mole Saddle via Bull Creek: 5 hours. Mole Saddle to Mataki Lodge: 3 hours.

Maps: Matakitaki M30, Murchison M29.

Access: From Murchison, take the Tutaki Road South to Mataki Lodge (about 35 km).

Alternative Routes: An easier and gentler trip than the one described below would be to go only as far as Mole Tops, either basing yourself at the hut or camping by one of the many tarns on top.

Information: Visitor information centre, Murchison, Ph 03 523 9350.

The Mole Tops and D'Urville Valley are situated at the western edge of the Nelson Lakes National Park, and see far fewer visitors than the more popular areas around St Arnaud. This tramp offers a mixture of gentle beech forests, expansive, tarn-sprinkled tops and excellent views across to the Nelson Lakes mountains. The wide-open alpine area can easily be reached along a good bush track from Tutaki Road South, and from the tops a variety of routes is possible.

The track up Jameson Ridge from Tutaki Road South is gained by following the north bank of the Mole Stream for a short while, then angling away uphill to the crest of the ridge. Walk below tall stands of red beech on a well-marked track, which is never too steep and climbs steadily to emerge at the bushline after two-and-a-half hours. The Mole Hut (a cosy, recently upgraded four-bunk hut) is situated back down the stream below, and is best reached by following the bushline eastwards for some 300 metres to a narrow stream basin, then heading downvalley nearly as far as the bush edge. The small hut is located on a narrow terrace above, on the true left of the creek.

If you intend to carry on into the Tiraumea Valley, continue up to Mole Saddle and bypass the hut. Poles mark the route from the forest edge to the broad, 1269-metre saddle, where a cluster of small boggy tarns nestles in a depression.

The actual Mole Tops lie south of the saddle and are worth exploring – the going in the main is easy tussock and scree across broad ridges and tarn-filled basins. In

Crossing the D'Urville River

summer, camping on these tops would allow more time to be spent here, and would also provide evening views across to the Mahanga and Travers ranges. With limited time, however, a quick circuit along the broad ridges to the south of the saddle offers excellent views over the ranges and down to Lake Rotoroa; allow three to four hours for this side trip from the Mole Saddle.

A poled route leads northwards from the saddle into the Tiraumea catchment, first along an open, tussocky ridge to the bushline, then down through pleasant beech forest to a river. The track does a lot more up and down than is apparent from the map, as it sidles above this tributary of the Tiraumea River, eventually dropping steeply to open flats and the tidy six-berth Tiraumea Hut. Allow at least three hours from Mole Saddle, and longer if you are tackling the route in reverse.

The track from Tiraumea Hut to the D'Urville River is a pleasantly gentle 150-metre climb. It passes initially through beech forest as far as the 672-metre Tiraumea Saddle, then heads more steeply down through a mixture of totara, matai and kamahi to the open valley floor.

The D'Urville Hut (ten bunks), by the shores of Lake Rotoroa, is a further half-hour down the valley, but our route turns south for a kilometre before heading up the first obvious side creek, coming in from the true left. This is Bull Creek, and it can be slow going as the track is no longer maintained, although it is marked from time to time. The route does, however, provide an interesting boulder-hopping and stream-crossing exercise in a pretty valley, leading back up to the Mole Saddle from the valley floor in about four to five hours.

At the saddle, pick up the poled route into Mole Stream, which can be followed all the way down to the road as an alternative to the Jameson Ridge route. After half an hour you pass the Mole Hut, from where the track enters the forest, generally following the true left bank of the stream to a crossing lower down. From here on, the going is easy by the river, before the path finally climbs up to a terrace and joins a broad farm track to the farm boundary fence. It is only a short stroll from here across paddocks to a final crossing of Mole Stream and a scramble up to the road below Mataki Lodge.

Lake Rotoroa from the Mole Tops

Kirwans Track

Duration: 2 days.

Grade: Moderate.

Time: 11–14 hours total. Capleston to Kirwans Hut (12 bunks,
stove with coal provided): 5–6
hours. Kirwans Hut to Kirwans Hill:
1–2 hours return.

Map: Reefton L30.

Access: At Cronadun, 11 km north
of Reefton on SH 69, turn onto
Boatmans Road; the route starts
at the roadend (6 km).

Alternative Routes: Continue
down the Montgomerie and
Waitahu river valleys to exit at the
Gannons Road bridge, then cross
the saddle to Capleston
(8–9 hours).

Information: DoC Reefton, Ph 03 732 8391.

WARNING! This was once a mining area – beware
of old workings, unstable structures and mine shafts.

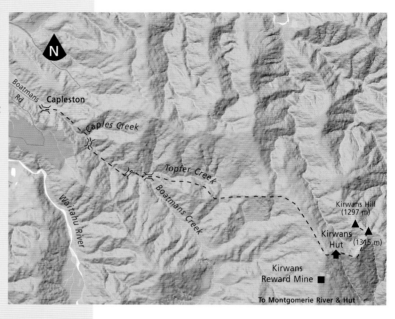

Kirwans Track offers a good introduction to the
less frequently visited Victoria Conservation Park,
situated west of the Main Divide between Reefton
and Inangahua. This range of rugged bush-clad
mountainsides and open tussock tops offers a
great weekend trip, with superb views over the Paparoas and down the crest of the
Southern Alps to Aoraki/Mt Cook. The whole district is steeped in history, being part
of the Reefton Goldfields Area. It saw 10 years of intense mining activity following on
from the 1896 discovery, by William Kirwan, of gold-bearing quartz high on the hill
now bearing his name. The existence of the fine Kirwans Track, which passes through
forest to a comfortable bushline hut, is due to the hard work and perseverance of the
early miners who searched for gold in the Inangahua/Reefton area.

The track starts at the now defunct goldminers' settlement of Capleston, 17
kilometres north of Reefton at the end of Boatmans Road. Back in the late 1800s these
grass- and gorse-covered flats apparently boasted seven hotels, built to support a population of over a thousand. The legacy of these industrious times lies scattered throughout the region in the form of various old mining sites, fenced-off shafts and drives,
derelict huts and batteries, and a perfectly graded pack track, which our route follows.

The initial 20 minutes from the roadend starts at a rotting wooden bridge over
the creek and passes along an old road line through farmland and into the forest.
The track leads down through a man-made tunnel, used to divert water from nearby

battery sites, before abruptly crossing Boatmans Creek on a long swingbridge to the true left bank. The gently undulating track now passes through fine specimens of the dominant red beech to cross, after about an hour, a substantial wooden bridge leading back to the true right bank. Shortly after this, the junction of Boatmans Creek and Topfer Creek is reached, and a further bridge crosses to the true left of Topfer Creek, where the track starts its long, steady climb up to the bushline.

This is an extremely well-graded path as it heads up the spur, sidling in and out of narrow side creeks, and with occasional zigzags up steeper sections to gain about 900 metres of elevation in three to four hours. Expect to be accompanied through the forest by friendly fantails, tomtits and bush robins, and if you are lucky you may also spot a shy kaka off the track.

As the bushline is approached, a clearing with an old ruined hut is passed before a side trail leads steeply uphill from the main pack track for 15 minutes (and not really the half-hour that is indicated) to the well-designed and spacious Kirwans Hut, complete with its large frontage of panorama windows. This 12-bunk hut (stove with coal provided) is located in a clearing on the 1294-metre-high Kirwans Knob, and has views on a fine day down the length of the Southern Alps to Aoraki/Mt Cook on the distant horizon, some 220 kilometres away. Closer at hand is the rugged Paparoa Range, rising above the Inangahua Valley to the west, with the southern outliers of the Victoria Range poking above the twisted beech forest around the hut. The obvious scar of the Garvey Creek Coal Mine to the southwest cannot be missed among the otherwise virgin ridges and valleys.

The open tops around Kirwans Hill provide an even better panorama and should

Hikers on Kirwans Hill with the Paparoas behind

not be missed so long as the weather is fine. The extra 45-minute walk from the hut is worth the effort, especially if you time it to enjoy a memorable sunset over a size-able part of the top half of the South Island. The track up through the final section of forest to a tussock- and scrub-covered ridge is straightforward, leading directly to a commanding high point at 1315 metres. The trig point of Kirwans Hill itself is slightly

Evening at Kirwans Hut, Victoria Conservation Park

lower and to the west of here, while an outlier summit at the eastern end of these limited open tops looks down to the forested depths of Kirwans Creek and the Mont-gomerie Valley beyond.

On a clear day the views from this isolated hill are stunning, from the obvious blocky top of Mt Owen, framed in a saddle to the north, down the rugged crest of the Victoria Range to Mt Rolleston at Arthur's Pass, Mt Evans and Mt Whitcombe at the head of the Wanganui River, and all the way to Aoraki/Mt Cook and its neigh-bouring peaks in the far south.

Remember to take a torch for the gloomy half-hour return trip through the forest back to the hut.

The Kirwans Track drops steeply from the hut to Montgomerie Valley and down to the Waitahu River, enabling a full circuit of the area to be made. The final 14 kilome-tres of this circuit follow a rather dull 4WD road, so returning along the previous day's ascent route is realistically a preferable, and much shorter, option. If you are planning on making the round trip, allow seven to eight hours to complete the circuit back to Gannons Road bridge, plus a further hour over the low, scrubby saddle to the start of the track at Capleston.

There are a number of interesting exploratory trips that can be made around Kirwans Hut, including the Kirwans Reward Mine, just a short distance below the main track over the saddle. The remains of an aerial ropeway with buckets attached can still be seen at these opencast workings, while further downhill the ruins of Mrs Flannigan's boarding house can be found in a bush clearing. Some time spent before-hand at the extensive and very informative displays at Reefton Visitor Centre will give a fuller perspective on the fascinating history of this region.

Lake Daniells

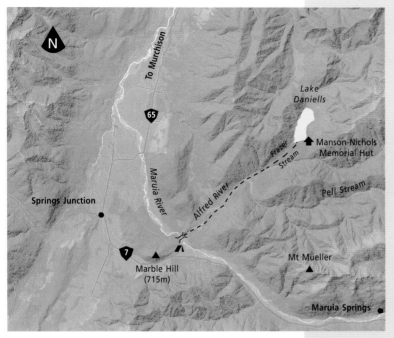

Duration: 2 days.

Grade: Easy.

Times: 6 hours total. SH 7 to Manson-Nichols Memorial Hut (sleeps 24, stove with coal provided): 3 hours.

Maps: Springs Junction L31, Lewis M31.

Access: SH 7, 10 km west of Maruia Springs. Pick-ups and drop-offs, plus safe car parking, can be arranged with Maruia Springs Thermal Resort, Ph 03 523 8840.

Information: DoC Reefton, Ph 03 732 8391.

The trip to Lake Daniells is a perfect introduction to the delights of getting away from the main highway for a night, and a good first tramp for enthusiastic children. The track through the forest is very gentle and leads to a comfortable hut by a tranquil lake, complete with a stove for cold evenings and state-of-the-art 'Rota-loos' instead of the usual smelly long-drop. A spot of early morning fishing from the boat jetty as mist drifts over the water completes the idyllic weekend away, although others may have the same idea and consequently the hut at Lake Daniells can get crowded.

The track starts at Marble Hill, 10 minutes' drive west of the hot pools at Maruia Springs. There are several DoC campsites within a few hundred metres of each other by the forest edge, a good place to spend Friday night before setting off for the lake the next morning.

The track is of a high standard all the way, mostly through delightfully lush beech forest interspersed with a few grassy river flats. Upon entering the forest, the track soon crosses a small bridge over the Maruia River, where the clear blue waters are funnelled through a narrow gorge. Alluvial gold has apparently been found here, giving this section of river the nickname the Sluice Box.

The track then follows above the Alfred River, passing beneath large stands of red beech where a mixture of broadleaf species, mosses and ferns smothers the forest floor.

Continue for an hour or so to a well-positioned bench, situated above the confluence of the Alfred and Pell rivers. Once, no doubt, this offered a view down to these forks, but forest growth has now obscured the outlook.

Soon after, the track leaves the Alfred River and follows the smaller Frazer Stream up to Lake Daniells. It is only a short distance around the lake to the Manson-Nichols Memorial Hut (sleeps 24, stove with coal provided), which is situated in a clearing with a fine view over the lake to forest-clad hills on the far shore. This hut is named in memory of three trampers, Brian and Sharon Manson and Phil Nichols, who died on the opposite shore in 1975 when the hut they were staying in was hit by a mudslide.

The way back is via the same track down to the highway, and takes between two and three hours. Allow for a leisurely morning's exploration of the nearby forest first, or rise at dawn to enjoy the early morning mist over the water, go fishing or even swim in the safe waters of the lake.

Lake Daniells, Lewis Pass National Reserve

Mt Mueller

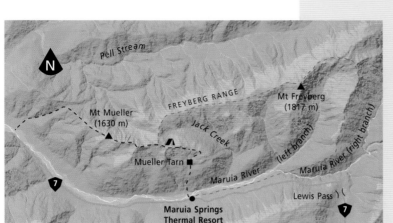

Duration: 1–2 days.

Grade: Moderate.

Time: 8–10 hours total. Maruia Springs to tarn camp: 4–5 hours. Tarn camp to Maruia Valley floor via Mt Mueller: 4–5 hours.

Map: Lewis M31.

Access: Near Maruia Springs, just west of Lewis Pass. Pick-ups and drop-offs, plus safe car parking, can be arranged with Maruia Springs Thermal Resort, Ph 03 523 8840.

Alternative Routes: Continue along the Freyberg Range to the east, before dropping down into the Upper Maruia Valley.

Information: DoC Reefton, Ph 03 732 8391.

This tramp starts and finishes near the Maruia Springs Thermal Resort, below the Lewis Pass, which provides weary trampers the chance of a welcome soak after they have explored the mountaintops of the Mueller Range. A mixture of forest, tarn-dotted tussockland and some rocky ridgelines make this readily accessible tramp a varied and worthwhile outing. It is quite possible to complete the round trip, as described, in one day, although a night spent camping by one of the ridgetop tarns will turn it into the ideal weekend break.

The start of the track is signposted some 200 metres west of the resort, where for a small fee cars can be safely left. After crossing the shallow Maruia River, a steep but well-marked track climbs away from the valley floor and heads directly up through mixed beech forest to the bushline. Mueller Tarn is a 600-metre workout above; remembering the rule-of-thumb calculation for speed of ascents (300 metres per hour across average terrain), this should take roughly two hours. The tarn is nestled in a rocky hollow at the bush edge, making a pretty lunch spot before you carry on to the open tops. There are secluded spots in among the forest nearby where a tent or two can be pitched.

The ridge above is gained by weaving through bluffs directly above the tarn, or by sidling eastwards onto the gentle spur overlooking Jack Creek. Upon reaching the top, scramble along the exposed schistose ridge and over Pt 1566 to a small tarn near the head of Jack Creek. This is an excellent fair-weather campsite if you intend to make this a leisurely two-day outing.

The ridge towards Mt Mueller is exposed and rocky in places, although steeper sections can usually be bypassed if necessary. Great panoramas are to be had in clear weather, of a profusion of forest-clad valleys and brown, undulating mountain ridges heading off in all directions.

From the trig beacon on the summit of Mt Mueller, a poled route leads down the ridge to the bushline, from where a good track descends through the forest to emerge at the shingle-smothered Maruia riverbed some 10 kilometres west of the resort.

An alternative, though harder, trip takes in the Freyberg Range to the north. Instead of climbing Mt Mueller, drop down to the saddle at the head of Jack Creek and follow the broad and rolling ridgetop to Mt Freyberg, with good views of Faerie Queene and Gloriana to the northeast. Water is scarce along this ridge, although a tarn just short of Mt Freyberg itself would make a fine campsite, about five hours from the suggested first day's camp on the Mueller Ridge.

The best descent to the Maruia Valley from here is via the broad spur to the east of the left branch of the Maruia River. This involves traversing over and around the craggy peaks to the north of Mt Freyberg and following the grassy spur to the bush edge, from where some careful navigation leads down to the river junction at the valley floor. (A direct descent down the left branch of the Maruia is not recommended, as there are extensive bluffs at the head of this valley.) This trip could be achieved in two longish days, and has the advantage of finishing near the initial start point, so you can walk directly back to the hot pools – a fitting end to any weekend tramp!

Mueller Tarn, Lewis Pass

Lewis Pass Tops

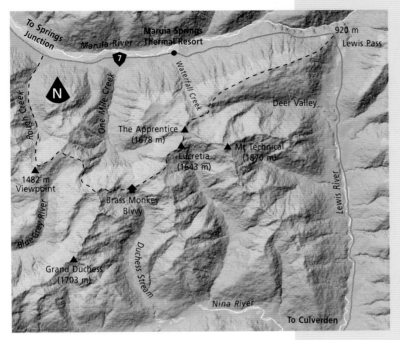

Duration: 2 days.

Grade: Moderate.

Time: 11–13 hours total. Lewis Pass to Brass Monkey Bivvy (2 bunks): 6–7 hours. Brass Monkey Bivvy to Lewis Pass Highway via Rough Creek: 5–6 hours.

Maps: Lewis M31, Trackmap 335/06.

Access: From SH 7, 500 m west of Lewis Pass (920 m). Pick-ups and drop-offs, plus safe car parking, can be arranged with Maruia Springs Thermal Resort, Ph 03 523 8840.

Alternative Routes: From the pass above the Blue Grey Valley, follow the poled route heading south down to the bushline and on to Lake Christabel Hut (2–3 hours). Return to the road from the hut (5–6 hours).

Information: Hurunui Visitor Information Centre, Ph 0800 442 663.

This classic tops trip in the Lewis Pass area is very accessible from the main highway and offers a fine tramp above the bushline with very expansive views for much of the time. A couple of rocky summits are climbed en route, and you have the opportunity of staying at a cute little tarnside bivvy hut. By starting near the crest of the Lewis Pass, at 920 metres, a lot of the hard uphill work is taken out of the trip. However, there is still enough to keep the hillclimbers happy, with the long descent reserved for the end of the tramp on the second day.

A signed track leads uphill from SH 7, 500 metres west of the Lewis Pass, passing through patches of open scrub and into mature beech forest to emerge at the well-defined bushline after an hour or so. Poles lead from here up onto the undulating ridge above, which is followed over a carpet of delightfully springy alpine grasses and a scattering of small tarns.

The route is unmarked after these tarns, but obvious enough in clear visibility, dropping over a rocky knoll to a saddle before climbing steeply up to The Apprentice. At 1678 metres this peak is the highest point reached on this tramp, and is about three hours from the highway. Mt Technical (1870 metres) can also be climbed from here. Its Northwest Ridge offers a fairly tricky scramble, although this can be avoided by

49

skirting above Lucretia Creek to the south until a suitable scree-filled gully leads directly to the top.

The route continues to the summit of Lucretia along the narrowing ridge, which is adorned with a few rocky towers along the way (these can easily be bypassed if necessary). Beyond this summit, with views across a large section of the Lewis Pass mountains and valleys, the ridge carries on in a southwesterly direction, over a couple of minor bumps, until an obvious tarn draining into Duchess Stream can be seen below. From this point, descend to a small, definite saddle occupied by some picturesque tarns and an orange-coloured 'garden shed'. This shed is the Brass Monkey Bivvy, which has recently been lovingly renovated by enthusiastic volunteers and now provides perfectly snug accommodation for two people. As its name implies, the north–south-aligned site is not basked in endless sunshine, and at 1300 metres the bivvy can get quite cold. Nevertheless, it makes an excellent overnight stop along the way. Note that toilets are not provided, so ensure that the area around these small tarns and One Mile Creek, which drains them, is kept free of human waste.

From Brass Monkey Bivvy there is a choice of routes around to the pass above Rough Creek. It is a strenuous climb from the bivvy back up to the ridgetop first thing in the morning, but with clear visibility this is a better option than the long sidle around the upper basin of One Mile Creek. This sidle crosses a few scree slopes and

Late evening, Lewis Pass tops

tussock shelves, before heading up to the broad ridge overlooking the Blue Grey River.

Once the first rocky lump on the ridge has been gained, the route then continues to Pt 1674, from where a ridge leads southwards to the popular summit of the Grand Duchess. Our route to the head of Rough Creek follows the increasingly narrow main ridge, with a scattering of avoidable rock towers. The final peak over-looking the Blue Grey River is quite craggy and steep to climb down; a better option would be to descend the gully that drops from just below the summit to the head-waters of One Mile Creek. A couple of small tarns are passed en route, before a short climb leads back onto the now broad ridge heading north.

Lake Christabel from Lewis Pass tops

The going is now considerably easier along this soft, grassy ridge, which curls around the head of the Blue Grey Valley to a high 'pass' above Rough Creek, about three hours from the bivvy. Drop your packs by the wooden pole marking the pass and stroll uphill for five minutes to a flat-topped summit overlooking Lake Christabel, nestled among a swathe of thickly forested ridges and valleys. This is a perfect lunch stop on a clear day.

The poled route over this pass is followed down and across the tussock basin at the head of Rough Creek to a well-marked track into the forest. The name is apt, as it is fairly steep and overgrown in places, but the track is always adequately marked as it follows one side or the other of the small creek, crossing frequently. The route is barred by sporadic tree falls, but it is easy to pick up the trail beyond these obstructions. The 900-metre descent from the pass back to the highway takes between two and three hours.

The track emerges from the forest five kilometres west of Maruia Springs Ther-mal Resort; if prior transport arrangements have not been made, it may be possible to hitch a ride along this fast section of road. Otherwise, allow 45 minutes for the walk back to the hot pools, by which time they will be appreciated even more.

Lake Man

Duration: 2 days.

Grade: Moderate.

Time: 13–15 hours total. SH 7 to Lake Man Bivvy (2 bunks): 5 hours. Lake Man Bivvy to SH 7 via Lake Man and the Doubtful Range: 8–10 hours.

Maps: Lake Sumner L32, Boyle M32.

Access: Lewis Pass Road (SH 7), 1 km north of Engineers Camp.

Alternative Routes: In poor weather you can cross the 1300-m-high saddle directly from Lake Man Bivvy to the Hope River instead of traversing the Doubtful Range.

Information: Hurunui Visitor Information Centre, Ph 0800 442 663.

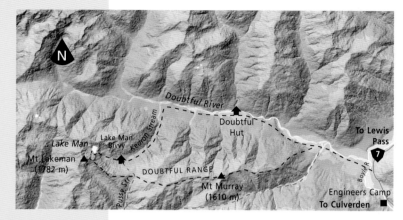

The trip to Lake Man lies slightly off the beaten track, which is probably just as well since the bushline bivvy sleeps only three at a squeeze. Combined with a return trip over the Doubtful Range, it is a classic weekend tramp, with a blend of river valley and mountaintop travel, plus a side trip to a wild alpine lake.

The trip starts by wading through the Boyle River about one kilometre west of Engineers Camp on SH 7 (cars can be parked more safely here than right by the side of the road). For anyone who is not yet a die-hard Kiwi tramper, it is possible to cross the Boyle barefoot, since the remaining 14 hours are potentially dry.

Gain a low terrace on the far bank and follow easy sheep tracks through thickets of matagouri on the true right of the Doubtful River. This track follows the river flats, with a few incursions into the beech forest, to reach the small and run-down Doubtful Hut (sleeps three) after about two hours. Continue along the flats for an hour to the junction with Kedron Stream, where a signpost points up to the bivvy. The track is initially steep but well marked through the thick forest understorey, before easing off to reach the cheerful orange tin shed that is Lake Man Bivvy some two hours from the valley floor. As the bivvy has only two bunks and floor space for one or two more, it is advisable either to carry a tent or arrive early on weekends.

Lake Man itself is about an hour above the bivvy, and makes an ideal side trip in the afternoon if you plan to return to the highway the way you came. Alternatively, a visit to the lake can be combined with the next day's travel, although this makes for a return trip of eight hours or more over the Doubtful Range.

A short section of forest and some bushline scrub soon leads from Lake Man Bivvy to easy alpine herbfields. Pass a waterfall on the true right before crossing above to gain a broad shelf that angles left towards the outlet stream of the lake. A short scramble up easy bluffs on the true left of the outlet waterfalls leads directly to the lake, a typical but nevertheless attractive alpine tarn set among towering crags and tussock slopes.

There are a number of possible routes from the lakeshore to the rocky ridge that culminates in the 1782-metre-high Mt Lakeman. Probably the easiest involves sidling around the lake for about 10 minutes before heading up tussock and scree slopes to the southwest. This soon leads to the crest of the ridge south of Mt Lakeman, which can be ascended via a rocky scramble from this point.

The ridge down to a broad saddle below (separating Kedron and Pussy streams) is quite sharp and exposed. It is possible to bypass most of the difficulties on the northern side, but care should be taken as the rock is quite loose in places. The springy alpine cushion plants that cover the slope down to the marshy and tarn-dotted saddle are a welcome contrast to the rocky terrain above. This is a good spot for some early lunch, as it is some three hours' steady travel from the bivvy.

A poled route leads directly from Lake Man Bivvy over this saddle to Pussy Stream and the Hope River. In bad weather this provides a more sheltered return route, although it is considerably longer than that over the tops: allow nine hours from here via the Hope Valley to the highway.

Early morning near Lake Man Bivvy

From a large tarn on the saddle, ascend the steep, broad hillside above to the main ridge of the Doubtful Range. This is easily followed, and affords great views to the north and south over Lake Sumner Forest Park and further afield. Mt Murray is reached after about three hours. From here, a tongue of tussock leads to the bush edge, where an untracked but fairly open route heads down broad, forested slopes to the sheep tracks along the Lower Doubtful Valley. You can then rejoin the previous day's track to return to the Boyle River crossing and the highway.

Lake Man Bivvy, Lewis Pass National Reserve

Buckland Peaks

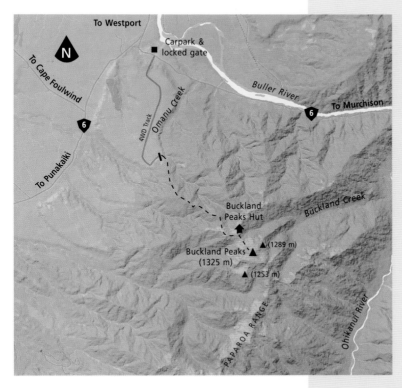

Duration: 2 days.

Grade: Moderate.

Time: 12–13 hours total. Carpark to Buckland Peaks Hut (6 bunks): 5 hours. Buckland Peaks Hut to Buckland tops: 2 hours. Buckland Peaks Hut to carpark: 3–4 hours.

Map: Westport K29.

Access: From SH 6, a few km east of SH 67 (Westport).

Information: DoC Westport, Ph 03 788 8008.

The Paparoa National Park takes its name from a range of rugged mountains situated near the West Coast, between Greymouth and Westport. Much of this area is accessible only to the hardened tramper, involving much trackless route-finding and serious rock scrambling along the sharp granite tops. The two Paparoa mountaintop walks described in this book, however, make forays into either end of the range, giving the moderate tramper a taste of the unique flavour of the region without the drama.

Their steep rise from sea level to over 1500 metres in a very short distance makes the Paparoas subject to rapid weather changes and, in summer, the tops invariably cloud over as the day warms up. Late autumn or even winter provide the visitor with more stable weather patterns without this daily cloud cover, and the crystal-clear views down the length of the South Island more than compensate for the shorter and colder days.

On SH 6, a couple of kilometres east of the Westport turnoff, is a sign to Buckland Peaks Track. The initial section of this walk is well-signposted and begins from a locked gate leading to open and uninteresting farmland. This is a case where your mountain bike would come in handy, cutting the approach walk of two hours down to just over half an hour of easy biking to the start of the track at the bush edge (leave your bike hidden in the bush, locked to a tree if you wish).

From here, the track climbs steeply through a short section of manuka scrub into the forest proper. The only water you pass until the hut is reached is a small stream on the true right of the the track near the start. The well-marked track meanders through mature stands of hard beech with a rich understorey of ferns. Higher up the hillside, the forest species include rata, kamahi and the unusual-looking mountain neinei, with soft, springy mosses underfoot. Listen out for the melodic song of the bellbirds, which seem to be quite prolific in this forest.

A 'halfway house' clearing in the bush provides a good rest stop, with fine views over the town of Westport and the Buller River winding its way towards the sea. A further hour or so through this delightfully varied forest brings you to the bushline and a section of subalpine scrub and tussock, with isolated pockets of forest largely comprising the locally common silver pine. The newly constructed DoC Buckland Peaks Hut (six bunks), which was built to replace the older Venturers Hut, soon comes into view, nestled in a sheltered basin below and to the northeast of the ridgetop. It is still common to hear great spotted kiwis calling in the forest at night near this hut.

If the peaks are cloud-free, drop your pack at the hut and continue up the ridge, following the marker poles. From here there are views up and down the top end of the South Island, and on a clear day the obvious snow-covered Aoraki/Mt Cook massif is visible to the south, at a distance of over 230 kilometres.

It is worth the effort making an early start for the Buckland Peaks themselves,

From Buckland Peaks, the view to the north, from Westport towards Karamea

Winter sunset on Buckland Peaks, with view northwards to Karamea

thus avoiding the frequent cumulus build-up that occurs on most days in summer. Climb up to a low saddle south of the hut and follow the broad ridge around to a second saddle. Ascend between interesting granite outcrops, with occasional rock cairns, to the high point of the Buckland Peaks, Pt 1325. Here, small tarns are tucked among strange rock formations and there is plenty of scope for exploration all around the open tops. In good weather it would be well worthwhile camping up here, where you can enjoy views south along the rugged spine of the Paparoas to the Southern Alps and north along the curving coastline towards Karamea.

    To return, follow the same track back down from the hut through the forest, taking care to spot the tree markers as several false leads could inadvertently be taken. The value of having a mountain bike at the bush edge will become even more apparent than on the ascent, as the final stretch is a pleasant downhill ride to the carpark.

Inland Pack Track

Duration: 2 days.

Grade: Moderate.

Times: 11–12 hours total. Carpark to Ballroom: 2–3 hours. Ballroom to Fossil Creek Camp: 2 hours. Fossil Creek Camp to Bullock Creek: 2.5 hours. Bullock Creek to Pororari River: 2 hours. Pororari River to Punakaiki road bridge: 2.5 hours.

Map: Punakaiki K30.

Access: Fox River carpark, SH 6. 20 minutes north of Punakaiki.

Alternative Routes: A quicker route back to the coast follows the Pororari River Gorge Track, which branches off the Inland Pack Track at a ford over the Pororari River.

Information: DoC Punakaiki, Ph 03 731 1893 – phone for up-to-date information on river flows before you leave.

WARNING! A good knowledge of safe river crossing techniques is important for this trip.

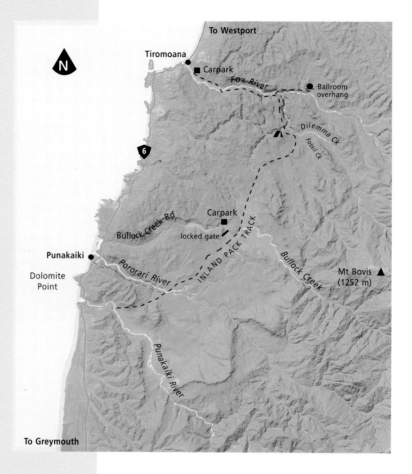

As you drive south from Westport along the winding and hilly coastal road to the start of this walk, remember that sections of the coastline here have been motorable only since the late 1920s. For the 60 years prior to the building of the road, access up and down this rugged stretch was possible only via a series of connecting pack tracks that ran some distance inland from the seemingly impassable coastline. Built in response to the opening up of the goldfields, the inland trails were never popular with the diggers, as they involved a great number of river crossings and bouldery valley floors that proved time-consuming for the laden ponies. Consequently, the tracks fell into disrepair long before the coast road was constructed, and only survive today by dint of the fact that they pass through some of the most unique and spectacular landscapes of the West Coast.

The attraction of the Inland Pack Track for trampers increases annually. A two-hour walk through this area of temperate rainforest and precipitous limestone gorges can bring you into the heart of some of the most impressive canyons in the country.

From the carpark immediately north of the Fox River bridge (Tiromoana), follow a well-marked trail into the forest and across dried-up riverbeds to where the track splits. A one-and-a-half-hour return detour is possible from here to the so-called Tourist Caves; torches are essential and be careful of stalactites at head height.

From this valley floor junction, the track crosses the broad but usually gentle Fox River to continue upstream on its south bank. If this initial river crossing presents difficulties then consider returning, since further crossings (there are plenty) will certainly be deeper and swifter.

Before plunging back into the forest, pause to look at the lower sections of the gorge, where majestic southern ratas rise above the canopy like giant heads of broccoli. One of these trees can be found by the water's edge as you emerge from the river crossing, its deep red flowers very characteristic of the West Coast forests in December and January.

The track contours above the river, with a few minor ups and downs. Remember to pause now and again to gaze up at the towering limestone walls overhead, complete with hanging gardens clinging to their precipitous sides. Soon the trail drops once

The Ballroom overhang, Fox River

more to the riverside, from where the Inland Pack Track cuts the corner of the Dilemma Creek/Fox River confluence.

If time allows – and it should – recross the Fox River before entering the narrow, green gorge just above the Dilemma Creek junction; this is a great swimming spot on a warm afternoon. Continue for half an hour up this delightfully secluded limestone canyon, with a number of wet-boot crossings, to reach a massive limestone overhang known affectionately as the Ballroom. There is enough room to sleep an army of trampers under this water-sculptured wave of rock, although in heavy rain the porous limestone does drip in places. A toilet is situated in the bush 20 metres away, firewood must be gathered only in the riverbed and resident possums will steal any carelessly stored foodstuffs once darkness falls. Nevertheless, the Ballroom is a bivouac rock par excellence.

If the rain arrives during the night, be prepared to sit out the high water rather than risk crossing a flooded river. Rivers in this area rise and fall very rapidly owing to the proximity of the Paparoa catchment area just 10 kilometres upstream, and patience in this respect could prevent a tragedy.

The route south towards Punakaiki follows the enticingly enclosed Dilemma Creek canyon from its junction half an hour downstream from the Ballroom. There is only one way up this narrow, picturesque gorge, involving wet boots during the numerous river crossings. The track is generally obvious, with

Pororari River canyon

limited opportunity to stray far from the river, although after periods of flooding there may be fallen trees and newly scoured pools to negotiate. A sign marks the spot where Fossil Creek enters the main gorge (there are good campsites here and even better ones further up the main valley), and the route follows this secluded and shady bare-rock streambed before climbing up to a dividing ridge separating the Fox and Bullock Creek catchments. Tall beech and rimu trees dominate this section of track. This is still limestone country, so do not stray from the marked trail since the lush undergrowth hides a multitude of potholes – as plenty of moas would testify, were they still foraging in these forests.

Eventually, the track emerges onto farmland (camping permitted), skirting swampy paddocks to a ford over Bullock Creek. From there it follows a short section of farm road before rejoining the track along an old logging trail. The mature forest of beech and rimu, with its rich understorey of ferns, mosses and lichens, makes the route over to the Pororari River a delightful complement to the rocky gorges so far encountered.

After fording the Pororari – easy in normal flow but impassable in flood – the true pack track continues southwards via a low saddle through pleasant sections of mixed broadleaf forest, before dropping down to the Punakaiki River. A quicker route back to the coast follows the Pororari River Gorge Track, which branches off the Inland Pack Track about 100 metres beyond the ford. This takes an hour and passes some inviting swimming holes along the way. The main route involves a gentle stroll along the left bank from the ford, which takes you to the road bridge, complete with the sound of West Coast breakers. Finish the tramp with a short walk along the road to Punakaiki township and a well-deserved coffee at one of the increasing number of cafés that have sprung up here in recent years.

Crossing Dilemma Creek, Paparoa National Park

Croesus/MoonlightTrack

Duration: 2 days.

Grade: Moderate.

Time: 12–13 hours total. Carpark to Ces Clark Hut (20 bunks, stove with coal provided): 4 hours. Ces Clark Hut to camp above Moonlight Valley: 4 hours. Camp above Moonlight Valley to Andersons Flat (21 km from Blackball): 4–5 hours.

Map: Ahaura K31.

Access: From Greymouth, follow the north bank of the Grey River to the Taylorville–Blackball road, then head to Blackball and the track end. There is an intentions book at the start of the track, which should be signed when entering the area.

Alternative Routes: Continue along the main Croesus Track to the West Coast, finishing at Barrytown, 15 km south of Punakaiki on SH 6.

Information: DoC Punakaiki, Ph 03 731 1893; DoC Hokitika, Ph 03 755 8301.

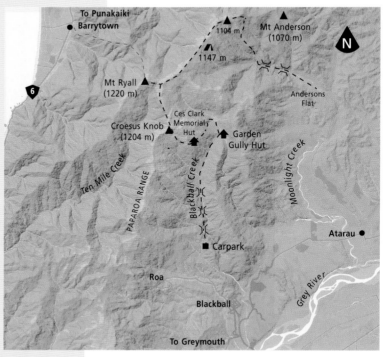

The Croesus Track is probably the best and most straightforward tramp up to the unique open tops of the Paparoa Range, which otherwise are generally not easily accessible. Although presenting some transport logistics, this is becoming a popular tramp at the southern end of the range as it is served by a network of good tracks and a large, comfortable hut. The trip described here is a variation on the normal Blackball to Barrytown route, taking in the less frequented tops to reach the Moonlight Valley. This has the advantage of being more of a round trip, providing another vehicle or mountain bike has been pre-placed in the Moonlight Valley.

Six kilometres above the historic town of Blackball is a large carpark and the start of the track, which follows up the Blackball Creek on a well-benched trail. Starting alongside an exposed coal seam and passing through a section of manuka scrub, the track soon crosses Smoke-ho Creek on a wire bridge and shortly afterwards drops down to Blackball Creek. A clearing marks the spot where the First Hotel was built in this now deserted valley. Things were very different in these parts during the mid- to late-1800s, when gold fever brought prospectors from all over the world in search of undreamed-of wealth. Along this stretch there are several campsite opportunities, if you do not plan to break up the journey at either the hut or the high camp.

As the Croesus Track is an old, established goldminers' route, all the rivers are bridged and it is well maintained, with relics of the bygone goldmining age scattered throughout the bush. In his book, *The Paparoas Guide* (1981, Native Forest Action Council; now sadly out of print), Andy Dennis writes: 'The track takes its name from the Croesus Mine, and the mine from the fabulously wealthy King Croesus of Lydia (now in Western Turkey) who ruled from 560–546BC. There was apparently an expression "rich as Croesus" and the miners who found quartz veins high on the end of this range were obviously optimists.'

The old and dilapidated Garden Gully Hut (two sagging bunks and an open fireplace) is located after some two hours of walking at a wide part of the valley occupied by swampy Lake Margaret. The hut is a couple of minutes from the main track and could be put to use if necessary, especially if you plan to explore the old stamping battery and mine entrance upstream. These relics are reached in about 20 minutes via a track and swingbridge over Roaring Meg Creek – the right fork climbs up to the mine mouth, while the left fork heads off to the old battery.

The forest in these parts consists of an interesting mixture of kamahi, rata, beech and neinei, among others, slowly changing to dracophyllum and olearia subalpine shrubs as the track gently zigzags up the hillside to the bushline. The Ces Clark Memorial Hut (sleeps 20, stove with coal provided by DoC), dedicated to a local who was the driving force behind the reopening of this old route to the West Coast in the 1980s, is reached after four hours from the carpark. Views from here on a clear day

The distant Aoraki/Mt Cook massif from near Mt Ryall

extend across the Grey Valley to the peaks of Arthur's Pass and the snow-covered Southern Alps to the south.

The track from the hut across the tussock tops past Croesus Knob to Mt Ryall (1220 metres) offers superb views in all directions. Note that although the route is frequently marked with plastic poles, it is quite exposed and therefore dangerous in bad winter weather.

Winter camp on a ridge above Moonlight Valley in the Paparoas

The main Croesus Track route to the West Coast leads back down from Mt Ryall into the bush, from where a good but steep path drops down a spur to a benched zigzag track through the forest. The track emerges onto the West Coast road directly opposite the Barrytown Hotel, about five or six hours after leaving the hut. It is just over 50 kilometres by road between these trailheads, which is rather too far for an easy bike ride back to your car.

However, instead of following the Croesus Track to Barrytown, this route gives an alternative way off the tops from near Mt Ryall without the same transport hassles. It involves continuing along the broad tussock ridge running northeast towards the central Paparoas until you are above the Moonlight Valley. The track is vague at times, although marked with the occasional pole. Good campsites are possible along this ridge, although water is scarce. There is a small tarn (unmarked on the map) just west of Pt 1147 that offers the best spot for an overnight camp, with great views over the Grey Valley and beyond.

Hopefully the morning views from this high ridge will justify bringing camping equipment, as the Paparoa tops are often clear at dawn and only cloud over as the day warms up. Continue along the ridge for a further hour to a low saddle and a DoC signpost pointing to the bush entrance at the top of the Moonlight Valley. The track through the forest is well marked as it drops steadily down the right branch of the creek, passing near the old Meikles/Moonlight Bivvy to cross a bridge in the main Moonlight Creek.

For the final couple of hours to Andersons Flat the track passes a number of old, rusting and overgrown relics from the goldmining days. There is even evidence of a small settlement, now largely reclaimed by the ever-advancing West Coast bush. From the route's end a rough forestry road leads down for nine kilometres to the main road near Atarau, and a further 12 kilometres to Blackball – a feasible proposition if you have a pre-placed mountain bike at Andersons Flat.

Mt Alexander

Duration: 2–3 days.

Grade: Hard.

Time: 16–17 hours total. Camp Creek Bridge to tarn camp: 6 hours. Tarn camp: to summit of Mt Alexander: 4 hours. Mt Alexander to Camp Creek Bridge: 6–7 hours.

Map: Lake Brunner K32.

Access: From SH 73, west of Jacksons Hotel, take the Inchbonnie–Rotomanu road as far as Camp Creek Bridge.

Information: DoC Arthur's Pass, Ph 03 318 9211.

Mt Alexander is the large bulky massif that you see rising up from across the Taramakau River as you drive between Aickens and Jacksons Hotel. The southern aspect of this range, as viewed from the main highway, presents a very steep escarpment that climbs directly from the valley floor, at an altitude of barely 200 metres, to the summit, at 1958 metres. The mountain has been climbed from this approach, but these days it is more commonly ascended from its gentler, western side.

Four to five hours of reasonable forest tracks lead to the rocky tops of the Alexander Range, from where a high camp by one of the many tarns provides a good base for a day or two's exploration of this fascinating area. These open tops provide a wonderful mix of weird rock outcrops, tussockland and wildflower-filled basins, plus a scramble along a shattered ridge to the actual summit of Mt Alexander, with its fine views across to the Arthur's Pass mountains.

The route up to the Mt Alexander tops follows Camp Creek, which is crossed some three kilometres beyond Lake Poerua on the Inchbonnie–Rotomanu road. A grassy track through a farm gate leads for 200 metres to a small building on the true right of the creek; cars can be parked next to this building, from where the track enters the forest over a stile. This track is overgrown with ferns in places, but there is a discernible ground trail following close to the stream. A small side stream is crossed

Evening camp by a tarn, Mt Alexander

before you enter a dried-up flood channel choked with large boulders. Beware of a false trail leading away steeply uphill from somewhere around here, as several parties have made the mistake of following old permolat markers up to a now derelict field station. To add to the confusion, the track on the topographic map at this point is drawn too high above the creek.

Instead, head up just above a second stream that enters from the true right. This leads up for some 200 metres before starting a long sidle high above Camp Creek. Although overgrown in places, the track is easy to follow and after an hour once again starts to descend to the main creek. You pass a rough-hewn sign before dropping abruptly, via an old rope and a new ladder, to the river. It is about two-and-a-half hours from the road to this point.

Cross to the true left bank, using the rope handrail if required, and clamber up a small slip to regain the track, which leads in a few minutes to an old tent camp. This is decidedly rough nowadays but could provide shelter if necessary. Shortly afterwards, a complex of private buildings owned by Landcare Research is reached (these are locked at all times). There are various tracks and associated markers in the vicinity of the buildings that can be misleading. Stay on the track that skirts below the field station, crossing two side streams before gaining a steep spur leading up to the main ridge.

This well-marked track weaves its way steeply through a forest of podocarps interspersed with tall stands of kamahi and rata. The characteristic mix of flax, toetoe and mountain neinei takes over as the bushline is approached at 1300 metres. Here, the forest and scrub abruptly give way to a jumble of large schistose rock towers decorating the crest of the ridge, reached in about two-and-a-half hours from the field station, which lies some 600 metres below.

There are a number of possible campsites on these tops, as water can be found in several grassy hollows, but the best spot is by a string of tarns located in an obvious fault depression to the southwest. These tarns lie somewhat off the proposed route to the top of Mt Alexander, but are definitely worth visiting as there are memorable campsites by their shores. They can be reached in less than an hour by following the rocky ridge and then descending steeply to the water's edge.

Retrace your previous day's route to the rock towers and continue eastwards along the broad ridge to the 1795-metre shoulder peak of Mt Alexander. In high summer, (January and February), this tussock ridge is blessed with a wealth of alpine flowers: the sunnier northern slopes are covered with dazzling clusters of the Mount Cook buttercup *(Ranunculus lyallii)*, while rich clumps of edelweiss *(Leucogenes grandiceps)* nestle among the rocky outcrops.

Should time or conditions dictate, this is a suitable turn-around point as the views from here are as good as any further along towards the main summit. Snow can lie along this final section of ridge well into summer, so care must be taken if you are continuing to the 1958-metre-high peak itself. It is probably easier to traverse along scree slopes on the northern side of this ridge; although the crest line presents a reasonable scramble over huge schistose blocks, the going is loose and exposed in places. Allow between three and four hours for the ascent from the camp to the summit.

The views from the top of Mt Alexander

Looking down on tarn campsites, Mt Alexander

are stunning. Strung out on the southern horizon, beyond the wide Taramakau Valley, lie the well-known peaks of the Arthur's Pass region, with Mt Rolleston to the north (left), snowy Mt Murchison further south and, on clear days, Aoraki/Mt Cook visible further down the unbroken chain of mountains. Far to the north, across the Grey River, lie the rugged Paparoas, while the expanse of

Schistose slabs on Mt Alexander

Lake Brunner occupies the lowland valley below this isolated summit on the western edge of the main Southern Alps.

The descent back to the road from lofty Mt Alexander is by the same route, involving a drop of over 1700 metres, and will take six to seven hours for those with good strong knees. Although it is possible to complete this trip in a two-day weekend, it would be far preferable to spend a second night at the ridgetop tarn camp.

Cedar Flat Hot Pools

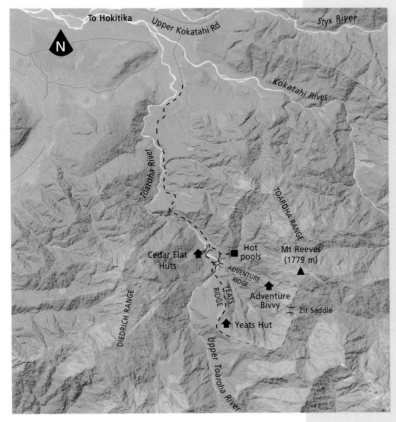

Duration: 2 days.

Grade: Moderate.

Time: 8 hours total. Toaroha Valley Road end to Cedar Flat Hut (6 bunks, wood stove): 4 hours.

Map: Kaniere J33.

Access: From Hokitika, drive through Kokatahi and along the Upper Kokatahi Road to a bridge over the Styx River, about 25 km from Hokitika. A small road leads off to the right 2 km beyond this bridge; follow it for a further 2 km to where it drops down to the Toaroha River. Park above this terrace — safely above potentially raised river levels!

Alternative Routes: Adventure Ridge Bivouac (2 hours each way) and Yeats Ridge Hut (3 hours each way).

Information: DoC Hokitika, Ph 03 755 8301.

The trip up to Cedar Flat is a relatively gentle affair, which is seldom the case on the West Coast.
The track is well marked and maintained throughout by DoC and is one of the easier and more accessible weekend trips from Hokitika. There is also the added bonus of hot springs only 15 minutes from the hut, although these frequently require some digging before they can be used and are not always as warm as weary trampers would like. Above Cedar Flat Hut more ambitious side trips can be tackled if time and energy allow.

From the Toaroha Valley Road end, follow the old tramway into the forest along the route marked with orange triangles. The original track by the river has been rerouted since the demise of sections of the riverbank, and now climbs some 200 metres to a spur. From here a steep descent leads, via a recent slip, to the bouldery Toaroha (allow about one-and-a-half hours to this point).

Three side creeks (usually easy to cross) enter the main river on the true right, after which the track turns abruptly away from the river to climb for 300 metres through dense stands of mixed podocarp and broadleaf species. It then levels out for the final gentle descent to Cedar Flat, the hut being visible through the trees from some distance away. A substantial wire bridge crosses to the south bank of the Toaroha to reach the new hut, which has six bunks and a wood stove. An older and very dilapidated hut nearby has two bunks and mattresses, and is a reasonable back-up in case of crowds.

Yeats Hut, above Cedar Flat

As the name implies, fine stands of the mountain cedar, or kaikawaka, a relatively common forest tree at lower levels on the West Coast, grow around the forest margins of the grassy Cedar Flat. The hot pools are located in Wren Stream and are reached by recrossing the wire bridge and following a newly cut track to a point about 200 metres above its junction with the Toaroha. The pools are a further 100 metres upstream on the true right and may require some minor earthworks in order to accommodate more than a solitary tramper. The temperature of this spring is also rather fickle, but during dry spells it provides a pleasant soak for weary muscles.

Even if time is limited to a couple of days, it is well worth exploring a short distance above the hut. The five-hour track to the Top Toaroha Hut leads, in about half an hour, to a small and attractive gorge in the main river, over which an airy swingbridge crosses to the true right bank.

There are two possible side trips that follow thickly wooded spurs up from the main river to the south and east: Adventure Bivouac (two bunks) takes about two hours to reach from the valley, while Yeats Hut (four bunks) is about three hours away. These tracks are a little overgrown, although reasonably well marked with permolat (sections of venetian blind; on the Yeats Ridge these come complete with encouraging remarks such as 'Go Back', 'Hut, 2 days' and 'Kiss this tree!', additions courtesy of, I presume, some distraught solo tramper!).

The bushline is typically rough, with thickets of leatherwood and flax, but soon tussocks and tarns make the going easier, and poles lead through subalpine scrub to the bivouacs. Both of these old Forest Service huts are situated above the bushline and have fine outlooks over the Diedrich and Toaroha ranges, as well as views down to Hokitika and the coast. If you have an extra day at your disposal, either hut would make an excellent overnight stay, with the promise of a West Coast sunset in clear weather. It is also possible to link up these tracks by traversing Mt Reeves from Adventure Bivouac to Zit Saddle, from where a route leads down to Yeats Ridge, although it would be a long day. This route is tricky in places requiring confidence on steep ground and good route-finding ability.

To return to Toaroha Valley Road end from Cedar Flat, follow the same route back.

Toaroha River en route to Cedar Flat

Mikonui Spur/Mt Bowen

Duration: 2–3 days.

Grade: Hard (route-finding skills required).

Time: 17 hours total. Totara Valley Road end to Mikonui Bivvy (sleeps 2–4): 7 hours. Mikonui Bivvy to Mt Bowen: 3 hours. Mt Bowen to Totara Valley Road end: 7 hours.

Map: Whitcombe J34.

Access: From SH 6, 3 km north of Ross, take the Totara Valley Road (4WD only).

Alternative Routes: An easier trip option, and a good first walk for aspiring West Coast trampers, would be to go only as far as the Mikonui Flat Hut (6 bunks). There are a number of longer, harder tramps possible from the Mikonui Valley.

Information: DoC Hokitika, Ph 03 755 8301.

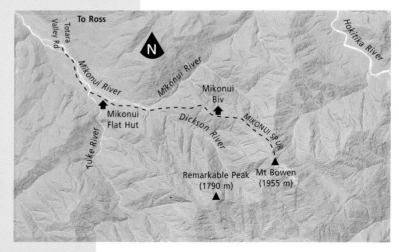

This trip gives a taste of West Coast tramping, with a romantic little bivvy hut to aim for after a day of varied and interesting hiking. It has all the ingredients of a classic tramp on this side of the Main Divide, complete with river crossings, easy valley flats, steep forest trails that require route-finding skills, and the inevitable subalpine scrub-bash before you reach the open tussock tops. All in all, this is a good introduction to the style of trip available throughout the entire West Coast region and a chance to hone up on those requisite bush skills.

The Totara Valley Road starts three kilometres north of Ross township and is suitable only for 4WD vehicles since recent floods destroyed two bridges over side creeks. These crossings now have passable fords, but check locally as to the current state of the 18-kilometre road to the Mikonui River.

Park by a tin barn and farmer's paddocks, next to the river. This is best forded straight away as the track on the true right has tricky sections before more open flats are reached. An hour of easy travel on grassy flats, including a crossing of the Tuke River coming in from the south, leads to Mikonui Flat Hut (six bunks), built on a terrace adjacent to the forest edge and easily missed when you are travelling up the valley. Mikonui Spur is the obvious bush-clad ridge that separates the main river from the smaller Dickson River, flowing in from the true left. The latter is crossed easily in normal flow to reach the base of the spur and forest edge. The track into the forest starts some 15 metres upstream from an old cattle fence and is marked with coloured tape at the bush edge.

Initially, the track is indistinct and rather overgrown, although well marked with tape tied to the bushes, and keeps close to a slip above the Dickson River. Soon, a better trail leads away from the river, once again marked with permolat and tape. It climbs steadily upwards through more open rata and kamahi forest for two to three hours, before the mature forest gradually gives way first to mountain neinei and then to thick stands of leatherwood scrub.

It is important to follow the vague ground trail through this belt of scrub, as it has become considerably more overgrown following the demise of a healthy deer population in these parts. Some do-it-yourself pruning of the smaller shrubs will help to keep the track open for other parties, as well as providing fresh markers for your all-important descent. Permolat markers still show the way through this dense section, where in places an obvious avenue of cutty grass and flax has in-filled the old cut trail.

Shortly before you reach Mikonui Bivvy, the ridge levels out as the scrub begins to thin. Skirt a short rise ahead and locate a rocky streambed on the true left, passing through a final stand of olearia and dracophyllum to tussock slopes above. It is easy to miss the small, faded orange bivvy in misty conditions, so keep a lookout for tape tied to bushes and the small tarn just below it. Built for two, the bivvy could sleep four at a push, although straws would have to be drawn for the two foam mattresses provided. Across the Dickson Valley stands the rugged Remarkable Peak, while downvalley the Mikonui River wends its way to the sea.

Above the bivvy a well-defined ridge leads southeastwards to the 1955-metre-high Mt Bowen. The track on this spur is surprisingly good, with a defined ground trail for much of the way. Steep sections along the crest of this ridge are easily overcome by the

Trampers on Mikonui Spur

usual method of scrub-pulling, and before long more open tussock and scree slopes are encountered. The final 300 metres to the summit are best taken up the obvious schistose scree basin to the south, skirting some rocky outcrops below the shattered peak of Mt Bowen.

On a clear day the wilderness extends an open invitation to travel further along these rugged tops. The options are many and varied, and a second night at the bivvy would allow for a leisurely day on these tops, but for a weekend trip the return is by the same route as the ascent. The descent is long and steep from the top of this West Coast peak, with a drop of some 1800 metres to the valley floor below. If you put a few temporary markers in place on the way up the Mikonui Ridge, then the descent should be a lot easier than the ascent, with gravity-assisted travel through the thicker sections of the bush.

Mikonui Spur, on the way to Mt Bowen

Scamper Torrent

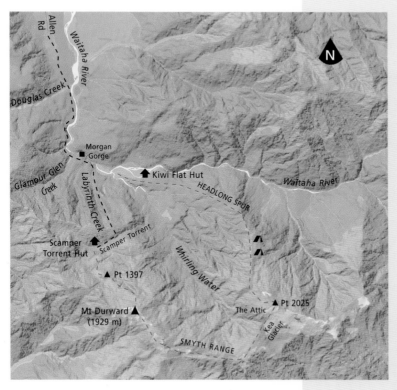

Duration: 2–3 days.

Grade: Moderate/hard (route-finding skills required).

Time: 14–16 hours total. Allen Road end to Scamper Torrent Hut (4 bunks): 7–8 hours.

Map: Harihari I34.

Access: From end of Allen Road, off SH 6 at Pukekura, 6 km north of Lake Ianthe.

Alternative Route: Ascent of Mt Durward, returning via Smyth Range and Headlong Spur. Allow an extra day for this trip, or 14–20 hours total (Scamper Torrent Hut to camp above Headlong Spur: 8–11 hours. Camp above Headlong Spur to Kiwi Flat Hut: 3–5 hours, depending on camp height. Kiwi Flat Hut to Allen Road end: 3–4 hours).

Information: DoC Hokitika, Ph 03 755 8301; DoC Franz Josef, Ph 03 752 0796.

WARNING! Side creeks can rapidly become impassable after heavy rain.

This is another classic West Coast trip, comparable to the Mt Bowen tramp (see page 72). The Scamper Torrent Hut is a snug little four-berth forest hut set in a pretty valley, with the craggy and complex slopes of Mt Durward rising directly above. The approach has all the right ingredients for a trip on the west side of the Main Divide: a rough access road, a boulder-hop along the Waitaha River, an impassable gorge to circumvent and a steep trail through thick forest to the tussock tops.

Starting at the small settlement of Pukekura, some six kilometres north of Lake Ianthe, take Allen Road up the true left of the Waitaha Valley. After about 12 kilometres the road deteriorates to a muddy track across farmland. The track into the bush starts at the top end of these paddocks, and is initially rather confusing owing to the maze of muddy cattle tracks veering off in every direction. Douglas Creek is reached in half an hour or so, from where the route upvalley boulder-hops along the Waitaha River as far as the lower end of the impressive Morgan Gorge. After crossing Glamour Glen Creek, the track climbs above the gorge, continuing in a familiar West Coast fashion with plenty of ups and downs through the forest to the continuous background roar of the enclosed river below.

Morgan Gorge is a typically impressive West Coast canyon, and can be safely viewed as you cross Anson Creek, which plunges over the lip of this sheer-sided cleft about 30 metres below the track. There is an extremely inaccessible hot spring issuing forth from the side of the gorge a short distance upstream from this point. Its location is given away by its smell, but an abseil from above would be required to reach the

Morgan Gorge on the Waitaha River

pool of, presumably, hot water – an interesting diversion for someone who has time to spare!

The track eventually drops down to Kiwi Flat, about three or more hours from the roadend, despite the rather optimistic old sign suggesting that two hours is sufficient. Halfway along this shingle river flat is the six-berth Kiwi Flat Hut, a useful night's stopover if you plan on making the round trip along the tops (see below). Before you plunge back into the forest, it is worth inspecting an old swing-bridge that crosses Morgan Gorge and provides access to the rugged Hitchin Range to the east.

Labyrinth Creek flows down to Kiwi Flat a short distance up the valley; the bush track to Scamper Torrent starts about 200 metres up this side creek on the true right, the entrance being marked with a white permolat cross. It is a fairly steady slog of some 800 metres up this spur, taking about three hours to reach the tussock tops. As there is no water until you get to some small tarns on the ridge, it is necessary to fill up your bottles before you leave Labyrinth Creek.

The track is fairly obvious by West Coast standards and is marked now and again, although confusion can occur where tree falls block the way – beyond these obstacles it is important to relocate the track. The telltale presence of leatherwood, flax and neinei heralds the subalpine zone as the track heads directly uphill to emerge onto tussock slopes with fine views back down to the Lower Waitaha

River Valley. From this point widely spaced metal poles lead over Pt 1125 and down to Scamper Torrent, home to at least one pair of blue ducks. In misty weather it is important to follow these poles to avoid the bluffs and scrub-cloaked 150-metre drop to the stream.

After the confines of the forest this open streambed is a delight, offering easy travel upvalley for 300 metres to Scamper Torrent Hut, which is sited on a small terrace above the river on the true left. The four-bunk hut is built in a great spot with views southwards to the ravine-cut slopes of Mt Durward, rising above. It is well maintained, having recently been painted, and comes complete with a kerosene stove and heater (bring your own fuel), as well as some pots, bowls and a plastic rain barrel.

The normal trip involves returning by the same route, which will prove only marginally faster than the ascent. The alter-

Tussock tops above the Waitaha Valley, near Scamper Torrent

native return route will take an extra day, ascending Mt Durward to reach the Smyth Range, Headlong Spur, Kiwi Flats and the Allen Road end. This round trip is graded as hard. It is well worth doing in good visibility, but would be a dangerous proposition in poor weather as many deep ravines cut the slopes of Mt Durward.

The almost 1000-metre climb up the fissured slopes of Mt Durward, which rises directly above Scamper Torrent, is quite a complex affair, but a few markers show the way into the scrub across the stream from the hut. Head off in a southwesterly direction to gain the ridge, climbing up to a point where it is easy to traverse around the head of two large ravines, and making your way from here over to Pt 1397. Next, head southeast towards the top of a prominent gully visible on the map, from where the summit can be approached more or less directly.

The Smyth Range stretches eastwards from Mt Durward, and compared with the route-finding challenges so far is a gentle affair. Since you are unlikely to be up here on a bad day, you'll be able to enjoy the sensational views as you cruise along these open basins and broad tops, with Mts Evans and Whitcombe dominating the eastern horizon. Across the Wanganui Valley to the south you can look into the Garden of Eden and Garden of Allah snowfields, whose large icefalls plunge into remote westward-facing valleys.

A short plod up the Kea Glacier leads over Pt 2025 and down to a broad shelf called The Attic. Suitable campsites can be found around here, leading towards tomorrow's route down Headlong Spur.

The final day involves a long but relatively straightforward descent along Headlong Spur to the Waitaha River track, and from here on to Kiwi Flat Hut (six bunks). The subalpine scrub holds no surprises, and once the track through the forest is located, the route is assured, although expect some windfall blocking the way. Headlong Spur eventually levels out as the river is approached and joins up with the main valley track to emerge shortly after onto Kiwi Flats, where the hut is located. From here, follow the first day's track back to the road – the final three hours of a very memorable West Coast tramp that should whet the appetite for many more adventures on this side of the Main Divide.

Scamper Torrent with hut on terrace above the river

Mt Adams

Duration: 2 days.

Grade: Hard/easy mountaineering.

Time: 15–16 hours total. SH 6 to bushline: 5 hours. Bushline to camp: 2 hours. Camp to summit of Mt Adams: 2 hours. Summit of Mt Adams to SH 6: 6–7 hours.

Map: Whataroa I35.

Access: SH 6, 12 km north of Whataroa and 18 km south of Harihari.

Information: DoC Hokitika, Ph 03 755 8301; DoC Franz Josef, Ph 03 752 0796.

WARNING! This is a fine weather trip and should not be attempted when it is raining or if the river is running high. The summit ice fields of Mt Adams require the use of crampons and an ice axe, although the crevassed glaciers can be avoided.

Mt Adams is a much sought-after West Coast summit, being a superb viewpoint that lies within one day's reach of the main highway. The 2208-metre-high mountain is situated on the edge of the recently gazetted Adams Wilderness Area. It commands unsurpassed views across the Barlow River to the Garden of Eden snowfield, while southwards runs a myriad of peaks, culminating in the bulky massif of Elie de Beaumont and with Aoraki/Mt Cook suspended on the horizon. Directly below this steep mountain lies coastal farmland, with Okarito Lagoon stretched out along the coast.

All in all Mt Adams is a peak to savour, but should definitely only be tackled with a settled forecast. There is little joy for anyone – except the most seriously deranged peak-bagger – in plodding up 2000-plus steep metres and then not be rewarded with a view!

As you drive south from Harihari, the bulky form of Mt Adams dominates the view down the coast. It is 18 kilometres to the Dry Creek (or Little Man River) road bridge and Mount Adams Lodge, from where a short dirt road leads off the highway and along the northern side of the river. Cars can be parked at the gate, so long as they do not block access up the valley along the private 4WD road.

Follow this farm track for 10 minutes or so before cutting down to the normally dry creek bed, which is reached via a short section of tutu scrub. If this riverbed has running water in it then the main creek may well be difficult, or even impossible, to cross.

Dry Creek River is actually something of a misnomer, and you should be prepared to cross and recross the main creek several times as the route heads up along this river, involving a fair amount of boulder-hopping. Trampers who seek a degree of comfort in the outdoors should consider wearing an old pair of boots for the initial two hours up this creek and then changing to a dry pair at the start of the climb, since the rest of the route is a dry-boot excursion.

On Mt Adams, with Okarito Lagoon below

The valley soon becomes confined by steep, forested hillsides on either side, with the route above the river now visible straight ahead. A couple of dry side creeks on the true left make upward travel easier than in the main channel; be on the lookout for occasional old cairns.

The second major tributary entering from the true right appears to be the main river, but in fact the main river does a very tight and secretive twist to the south and is not visible from the junction. Follow up this side creek, which appears to lead to impassable bluffs. After some 100 metres, a large, moss-covered cairn marks the entrance into the forest on the true left and up the very steep spur above. Allow about two hours from the road to the start of the forest track. The water in this creek is the last until you reach the snowline, so be prepared to add a few kilos to the weight of your pack for the rest of the climb, or travel fast in order to reach any snow patches (found only near the top of the mountain in late summer).

A permolat marker shows the way into the bush, from where a generally good track climbs very steeply up a tree-root staircase away from the river. It takes about 20 minutes to reach the crest of the spur, at which point the track levels out for a short distance as it weaves a route through impressive stands of old rata trees.

The track soon steepens again but remains obvious, and as maintenance is somewhat haphazard, it is important to carry out a little shrub-pruning on the way for other parties, as well as to provide markers for your descent. Once into the subalpine scrub zone, the going gets a little tougher for half an hour or so, through the usual dense thickets of flax, astelia lilies and leatherwood, although a ground trail is always present. There is a suitable flat spot for camping near the start of this section, under a canopy of dracophyllum trees.

After some three hours from the valley floor the open tussock ridge is reached, where there is a good, cleared and levelled campsite right by the track. If time is running short it is best to stop here, but the summit of Mt Adams is still a long way off. Also bear in mind that afternoon clouds frequently obscure the lower slopes of these coastal foothills; the higher up a camp is sited, the better chance you have of being above it all.

The narrow, open ridge is easy to follow as it weaves its way through alpine meadows, which in summer are smothered in an array of buttercups, daisies or gentians, depending on the month. There are some steeper sections over the occasional rocky knoll, and in places the drop into McCulloughs Creek is precipitous and close to the track. Caution is needed here in icy conditions.

Suitable camping spots become scarcer, but a dried-up tarn bed to the north just below the ridge has plenty of level spots and, with luck, the odd snow patch. This is about two hours from the bush edge camp previously mentioned, situated at about 1700 metres and a short distance before the final climb to the shoulder peak of Mt Adams (Pt 2101). Once camp has been established, it is well worth heading up to the shoulder peak for sunset views over Okarito Lagoon and the West Coast (the descent back to camp takes just half an hour from here).

Above the camp a short section of ridge leads to an open rocky slope that continues up to the shoulder peak. Views from here are excellent, but the main summit

The Southern Alps in evening light, from Mt Adams

– 100 metres higher and a further half-hour to the west – commands even better views across to the Main Divide of the Southern Alps. Northwards, the obvious bulky mass of Mts Evans and Whitcombe fill the horizon, to the east the great tumbling icefalls of the Garden of Eden pour down between bare rock peaks, and southwards the unbroken chain of the Southern Alps extends past Elie de Beaumont to Aoraki/Mt Cook. The large West Coast valleys of the Perth and Whataroa lie in the shady depths of the morning light, while the coastal lowlands, dotted with small kettle lakes and bigger lagoons, lead the eye to an endless expanse of ocean. This must be one of the finest viewpoints on the coast that can easily be reached without the need for serious mountaineering skills.

The return to the road is by the same route, only considerably faster. The steepness of the ridge is more fully appreciated in descent, both visually when looking down and physically when your knees start to complain. Near the end of the enclosed river valley section of Dry Creek there is a fine little swimming hole for those warm summer afternoons, or you can wait for the hot pools in the Lower Wanganui River; either option makes a fitting end to a very memorable weekend on the West Coast.

Sunset from Mt Adams

Castle Rocks Hut

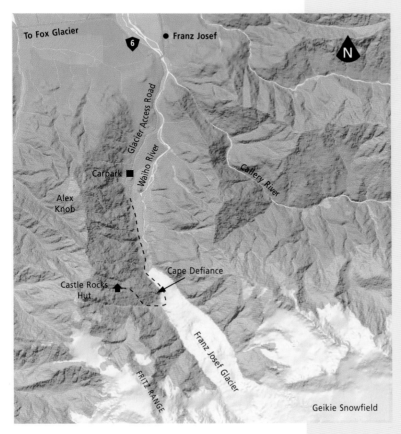

Duration: 2 days.

Grade: Moderate (crampon and ice-axe skills necessary).

Time: 7 hours total. Carpark to Castle Rocks Hut (sleeps 4): 4 hours.

Maps: Franz Josef G35, H34/35.

Access: Glacier Road along the west bank of the Waiho River from Franz Josef township.

Information: DoC Franz Josef, Ph 03 752 0796.

This trip to an historic hut perched above the famous Franz Josef Glacier is an ideal introduction to the delights of glacier travel, minus the risks of hidden crevasses. It does, however, require crampons and an ice axe plus the knowledge of how to use them. Nevertheless, the lower sections of the Franz Josef generally offer fairly straightforward travel on white ice, with routes well marked and steps cut by the guiding companies that operate all the year round on this glacier.

Follow the easy track to the snout of the glacier and pick up the easiest route onto the ice. This is usually on the true left, and should be quite obvious as guided parties also access the ice at this point. The route upwards, past the first icefall, will vary with conditions, but stays towards the true left with a brief foray out into the middle of the glacier. The rocky spur of Cape Defiance is passed after about two hours of travel; the bouldery gut directly above this spur is the route up to the hut.

Leave the glacier below the gut, which generally involves an easy stroll off the

83

smooth, white ice, although this will vary depending on the ebb and flow of the glacier. Scramble up the scree slope issuing from the gut, and ascend steeply the loose, rocky creek above. Occasional cairns mark the way (though the route is largely unmarked), passing an obvious large rock, before veering to the true left up a subsidiary valley. Care needs to be taken here, as the slope is very loose in places, although a vague trail zigzags up to marker posts showing the way to the hut. Castle Rocks Hut (four bunks) is sited on an old glacial terrace with views over the tumbling chaos of the upper sections of the glacier and to the surrounding peaks.

The Franz Josef Glacier was so named by the explorer Julius von Haast after the then Austro-Hungarian emperor, although local Maori had a far more poetic and poignant name for this river of ice. Ka Roimata O Hine Hukatere translates as 'the Tears of the Avalanche Girl' and refers to the tears shed by a Maori princess after her lover's untimely death among the cold and dangerous mountains into which she had led the unsuspecting lowlander.

In springtime, the subalpine flora that surrounds the hut offers an added dimension to this surprisingly seldom-visited part of the park. Directly above the hut are the tower-like Castle Rocks, where scrambling routes give access to the ridge, although care should be taken as loose rocks abound in this area.

Return to the carpark by the same route.

Castle Rocks Hut and Franz Josef Glacier

Mt Fox

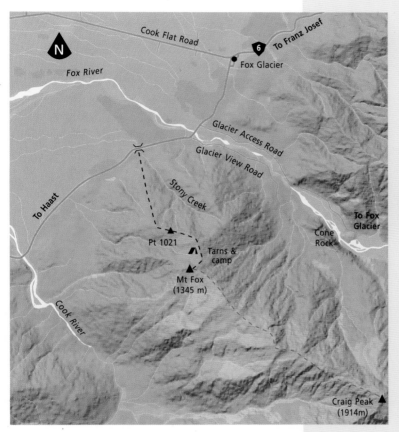

Duration: 2 days.

Grade: Moderate.

Time: 8–12 hours total. Thirsty Creek to Mt Fox: 3–4 hours. Mt Fox to ridge camp: 1–2 hours.

Map: Aoraki/Mount Cook Alpine Area special map.

Access: SH 6, 3 km south of Fox Glacier township (park just beyond Thirsty Creek culvert).

Information: DoC Fox Glacier, Ph 03 751 0807.

Mt Fox commands views second to none over the coastal plains of the West Coast and the Fox Glacier, from its terminal to the Upper Névé, and to the highest peaks of the Southern Alps. Despite being within easy reach of the highway, this unfrequented ridgetop seems surprisingly neglected. One possible reason for this is the almost inevitable afternoon cloud build-up that occurs around the West Coast mountains, particularly in summer, and denies many day hikers the views they came for. The best way around this is to plan a camp on the gently rolling Mt Fox–Craig Peak ridge. The heavier packs and associated effort involved with this is more than rewarded with evening and morning clearances across to peak after stunning peak.

Mt Fox rises above the broad, forested hillside just south of the glacier; the track starts three kilometres south of Fox Glacier village at Thirsty Creek (referred to as Stony Creek on the topographic map). A well-signed track from here ascends the thickly forested spur, which involves some steep scrambling up tangled tree roots and sections of rock, plus clambering over, under or around occasional fallen trees.

The forest in these parts is a delightful blend of rata and kamahi, along with some fine stands of the West Coast podocarp species, in particular rimu and miro. Towards the bushline, mountain neinei (commonly known as the pineapple tree) and flaky-barked tree daisies become abundant, and there are occasional large kaikawaka, or New Zealand cedars. If you are lucky, a fantail or two may accompany you through this forest, no doubt lured more by the insects disturbed by heavy tramping boots than any feelings of sociability. Listen out for the distinctive song of bellbirds, the noisy, somewhat clumsy flight of native wood pigeons and, as you near the tops, the unmistakable cry of the kea.

Mt Tasman and Aoraki/Mt Cook from ridge near Mt Fox

This steady climb through the forest takes about two hours to the trig point, situated among subalpine dracophyllum, leatherwood and flax scrub. The views are somewhat restricted here, as the mountains are still hidden behind the broad, scrub-covered ridge rising up to Mt Fox itself at 1345 metres. It takes another hour and a half along a well-poled track to reach the summit, which offers a fine view over the entire area. The narrow coastal strip to the west is covered with fields and a scattering of dwellings, and is bisected by the wide, braided Cook River as it wends its way to the Tasman Sea. Note the obvious sinuous forested ridges that roughly parallel the present course of the river; these are old lateral moraines left behind when far mightier glaciers than today's remnants flowed down from the Southern Alps to beyond the present coastline.

The tussock tops are transformed in the summer months to beautiful alpine gardens, with a scattering of white-flowering daisies (*Celmisia* spp.), mountain foxgloves *(Ourisia macrocarpa)*, Mount Cook buttercups *(Ranunculus lyallii)* and many other herbs that lie hidden among the protective tussock grasses.

As the top of Mt Fox is approached, the snow-covered mountains begin to rise tantalisingly above the intervening hillsides. This must be one of the finest views of the famous summits of the Aoraki/Mount Cook and Westland/Tai Poutini national parks, with the ever-dominant bulk of Mt Tasman, New Zealand's second-highest peak, soaring directly above the grassy ridges in the foreground. (For seriously purist mountaineers, it is possible to climb the full West Ridge of Mt Tasman via Mt Fox, starting at SH 6 and traversing a number of subsidiary summits before reaching the main goal, although achieving this would take an experienced party at least three to four days.)

Dotting this broad, undulating ridge are a number of post-glacial tarns, the shores of which would make an idyllic campsite with unforgettable views. There is a cluster of three or more tarns around the 1200-metre contour, but the views do improve the higher you go and more waterholes can be located further along this ridge; alternatively, you can use winter snow patches as a water supply if any are still lingering here.

The Upper Névé of the Fox Glacier, with its tumbling icefall, can be looked into directly from these high camps, with the blade-like Mt Douglas and flat-topped Mt Haidinger dominating the horizon. Further south, the crest of the Southern Alps rises ever more dramatically, over Mts Haast and Lendenfeld to Mt Tasman, and with the wide West Face of Aoraki/Mt Cook set slightly behind. Travelling southwards, the eye alights on La Perouse, the tops of Mts Footstool and Sefton sticking up behind the foreground ridges, and way to the south Mts Dechen and Hooker in the Landsborough Valley, framed by a low saddle.

You can now settle down in your camp for a quiet sunset, happy in the knowledge that you are not part of the hordes far below at Lake Matheson. The four-hour effort to reach this special place on the West Coast is most assuredly worthwhile.

Fox Glacier and the Southern Alps from Mt Fox

Set your alarm for sunrise, as this will produce a different, but equally memorable, spectacle of light and shadow from the previous night's sunset.

The return is by the same way, but an ascent of Craig Peak (1914 metres), the natural culmination of the Mt Fox ridge, would round off a great trip (note that crampons and an ice axe are sometimes required). Craig Peak gives yet more uninterrupted vistas of these 'ice islands lying off the coast', as the early explorers Thomas Brunner and Charles Heaphy described their first sighting of this 'Land Uplifted High'.

Winter camp on snow, on ridge above Mt Fox

Sawcut Gorge

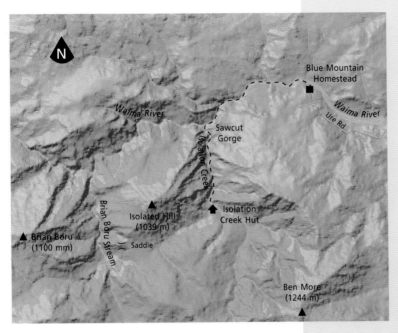

Duration: 1 day.

Grade: Moderate.

Time: 5 hours total. Blue Mountain Farm to Sawcut Gorge: 2 hours. Sawcut Gorge to Isolation Creek Hut (6 bunks): 30 minutes.

Map: Grassmere P29.

Access: Turn off SH 1 at the Waima Road Bridge, 75 km north of Kaikoura and 56 km south of Blenheim, for the 12-km drive to Blue Mountain Homestead.

Alternative Routes: Ascents of Isolated Hill or Ben More.

Information: Kaikoura Visitor Centre, Ph 03 319 5641.

WARNING! In heavy rain or when river levels are high this trip is best avoided, as the crossings can become tricky, if not impossible.

This is an interesting and varied tramp only an hour's drive north of Kaikoura, starting 12 kilometres inland from the main highway. The Isolated Hill Scenic Reserve in the Seaward Kaikouras has some unexpectedly dramatic scenery that lies within easy reach of the roadend, including the short but very spectacular Sawcut Gorge, which exhibits some memorable natural rock architecture. There are plenty of swimming opportunities along the way, so allow extra time for a dip on hot summer days.

Turn off SH 1 immediately after the Waima River Bridge and follow the gravel road for 12 kilometres to the farm at the roadend. Cars can be left here – enquire at the house and enter your name in the visitor's book.

A farm track descends to the Waima (or Ure) River, which is followed upstream into a steep-sided, narrow valley. This is definitely a wet-boot trip, since the river is crossed and recrossed many times as the route meanders up the shingle- and boulder-strewn valley floor. The smooth white limestone blocks provide some enjoyable rock-hopping, although they can be avoided if you prefer. Several small waterfalls and associated plunge pools are passed, when careful comparisons can be noted for the return swimming stops.

After about an hour the valley narrows into the first gorge near the junction with Headache Stream, at which point the track weaves among large boulders and remnants of forest podocarps. Species such as totara, miro and matai, along with red and silver beech and fine examples of kowhai, all grow in the narrow confines of the steep-sided gorge, while below the river is squeezed between giant tumbled blocks into a series of waterfalls. On the steep valley sides, look out for the Marlborough rock daisy (*Pachystegia insignis*), a species unique to this region of the South Island.

Sawcut Gorge, in the Seaward Kaikouras

After returning briefly to the stony riverbed, the track crosses back to the south side of the valley and enters Isolated Hill Scenic Reserve. Look out for the smaller Isolation Creek, which flows in from the south (true right) as the track up to Sawcut Gorge leaves the Waima Valley just upstream from the confluence.

At first sight it appears as if there is no feasible route through the steep cliffs ahead, but a narrow split in what appears to be the valley headwall leads you directly into a sculptured wonderland of water-eroded limestone. At times barely four metres wide, this cleft, cut through millennia of sea-floor deposits, soars up for some 50 metres to the narrow strip of sky and greenery above. Around the middle of the day in the summer months, sunlight filters down into the gorge, bouncing golden-yellow light off its curving sides while illuminating patches of the shingle floor.

The stream that flows through the 50-metre-long gorge is generally no problem to wade, beyond which the route continues with ease up the valley for half an hour to the six-bunk Isolation Creek Hut. Although not as spectacular as the gorge below, the narrow canyon bounding Upper Isolation Creek is still well worth a visit. The hut is sited on a broad terrace, just above a major fork in the valley.

A number of side trips are possible from here, especially if you plan to stay overnight at the hut. These include ascents of Isolated Hill or Ben More, which at 1244 metres is the highest coastal mountain in this area.

The return to the roadend is by the same route, taking time to sample a few of the swimming holes en route.

Mt Fyffe

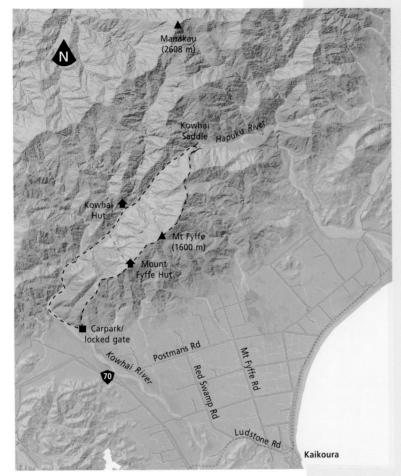

Duration: 2–3 days.

Grade: Moderate

Time: 12.5–14.5 hours total. Carpark to Mount Fyffe Hut (8 bunks): 2.5 hours. Mount Fyffe Hut to Kowhai Hut (6 bunks) via Kowhai Saddle: 7–8 hours. Kowhai Hut to carpark : 3–4 hours.

Map: Kaikoura 031.

Access: From Kaikoura township, drive 15 km along Ludstone Road and Red Swamp Road to Postmans Road; park at the roadend.

Alternative Routes: A descent of Spaniard Spur from Mount Fyffe Hut would shorten the trip considerably. The Hapuku Valley provides a different route back to SH 1.

Information: Kaikoura Visitor Centre, Ph 03 319 5641.

The Seaward Kaikouras conjure up visions of large, rolling mountains covered with endless slopes of scree and not a drop of water apart from the shimmering Pacific Ocean on the eastern horizon. Although parts of the range certainly live up to these expectations, there are some lush, bush-clad valleys separated by tussock- and shrub-covered ridges. Mt Fyffe is an easily accessible summit with a cosy little hut passed en route. The views from the tops are superb, encompassing a wide stretch of the east coast, from Banks Peninsula in the south up to the North Island. The Kaikouras have the added appeal of being on the drier east coast, away from the high rainfall that occurs west of the Main Divide.

Stormy sunrise from Mt Fyffe

Starting at the carpark at the end of Postmans Road, an easy 4WD track (locked gate) follows the ridge line directly to Mount Fyffe Hut; the hut is not marked on the topographic map, but lies just northeast of Pt 1103. This walk would even be quite feasible in the dark. (An alternative, and steeper, route is via the Fenceline Spur Track, which comes out on the road just 300 metres below the hut; allow three to four hours for this option.)

Mount Fyffe Hut is situated at a spectacular point on the ridge, with extensive views over the Kaikoura Peninsula and township. It has eight bunks and camping spots, and is ideally positioned if you want to watch the sun come up over the ocean.

The 4WD road continues for 1.5 hours all the way to the summit of Mt Fyffe itself, which at 1600 metres is the highest point along the coast here. A broad, scree-covered ridge with fine views across to Manakau, the highest peak in the Seaward Kaikouras, leads easily via a few ups and downs from Mt Fyffe to Gables End. From here, a steep shingle slope heads down to Kowhai Saddle, which separates the Hapuku and Kowhai catchments. Although it is possible to descend either valley, the preferred option is the latter, since it leads back to the start of the tramp without the need for prior transport arrangements.

It takes about four hours to reach Kowhai Saddle from Mount Fyffe Hut, and a further three or so to descend the surprisingly rough upper reaches of the valley to Kowhai Hut (six bunks). Occasional cairns mark the descent into the narrow and rocky streambed, which is followed downvalley using a combination of boulder-hopping interspersed with easier walking along sections of river flats. The welcome sight of Kowhai Hut, up on a small terrace, appears on the true right, shortly after the main

Kowhai River junction.

The walk out from Kowhai Hut is straightforward unless the river is running high. The bed of the lower Kowhai River is smothered in great piles of shingle, a result of a major flood at some time in the not-too-distant past.

Shortly upvalley from the confluence with Snowflake Stream a track descends steeply from the Mt Fyffe ridge to the east. This is Spaniard Spur, which leads down from near Mount Fyffe Hut and offers a much shorter, though less varied, trip than the route described. The track is well marked but steep; allow two hours from the hut to the valley floor.

There is a small gorge just below the Snowflake confluence, where several crossings of the main river are necessary; under normal flow these present no problems. Finally, you pick up an old vehicle track that leads back to the Postmans Road carpark.

Rainbow over Mt Fyffe Hut

Packhorse Hut/Mt Herbert

Duration: 1–2 days.

Grade: Easy.

Time: 4–6.5 hours total. Gebbies Pass to Packhorse Hut (8 bunks, wood stove with fuel generally provided): 2.5 hours. Packhorse Hut to Kaituna Valley: 1.5 hours. Packhorse Hut to Diamond Harbour via Mt Herbert: 4 hours.

Map: Lincoln M36/37.

Access: By road from Christchurch, via Governors Bay and Teddington to Gebbies Pass.

Alternative Routes: An excellent, although longish, day trip starts from Diamond Harbour, which can be reached via ferry from Lyttelton (regular service during daylight hours). The route ascends Mt Herbert before following the open tops to Mt Bradley, and heading from here down to the Packhorse Hut and back to sea level via Orton Bradley Park. There is a 6-km road walk back to Diamond Harbour and the Lyttelton ferry. Allow 8 hours for the entire trip. Trampers wishing to traverse Banks Peninsula as far as Hilltop, above Akaroa, can link up from Packhorse Hut with the private Sign of the Kukupa Hut (6 bunks, locked at all times, Ph 03 349 3607 for bookings), just below Waipuna Saddle near the Port Levy–Little River road.

Information: DoC Christchurch, Ph 03 379 9758; Lyttelton ferry enquiries, Ph 03 366 8855.

WARNING! The walkways in this area frequently cross private land, and are closed to the public during the lambing season, generally early August to late October.

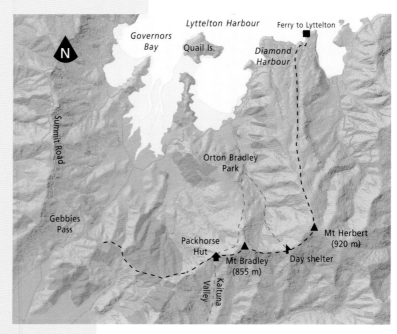

The historic stone Packhorse Hut has recently been renovated by DoC, and now boasts a new wooden floor, new bunks and a wood-burning stove. The Sign of the Packhorse was originally constructed during World War I as one of four roadhouses linking Godley Head with Gebbies Pass, designed to provide refreshments for city-dwellers out enjoying a hike in the Port Hills. The Christchurch visionary Harry Ell was responsible for the creation of the Summit Road Walkway, which was part of his ambitious plan to extend a track as far as Akaroa.

This straightforward hike is a perfect introduction to the delights of overnight tramping for children and adults alike. It is within easy reach of Christchurch and yet feels quite remote and above it all, especially when easterly clouds roll over the hills to envelop the cosy hut in wreaths of mist.

There are a number of possible hikes to and from the Packhorse Hut, and for those with the time and energy a trip incorporating Mts Bradley and Herbert would add considerably to the experience. It is quite possible to reach Diamond Harbour from Christchurch via the Lyttelton ferry, which makes a pleasant change from the usual long drive to the mountains.

If you arrive by car, it is best to drive a little way up the 4WD track (gate not locked) at Gebbies Pass and park safely out of sight of the main road. The track is well marked with coloured posts as it skirts, and then enters, the pine plantations that cover much of this side of the hill. Above this man-made forest, angle up through small pockets of surviving native bush, important remnants of the extensive podocarp/broadleaf forest that once covered much of Banks Peninsula in pre-European times.

The track then skirts below some very distinctive geological structures known as the Remarkable Dykes. These rock walls, which run vertically down the hillside, are igneous intrusions forced up through the earlier volcanic rocks that make up the majority of Banks Peninsula. The enormity of the Lyttelton Volcano, which erupted 10 to 12 million years ago, can be better appreciated from these heights, its huge crater now flooded by the murky waters of Lyttelton Harbour and its encircling crater rim still very much in evidence.

Shortly after it passes below the Remarkable Dykes, the track climbs up to the tussock-covered Kaituna Pass, where the sturdily built Packhorse Hut nestles below craggy hills on either side. Leave your pack here and enjoy an evening stroll to the small summit south of the pass, with views over Lake Ellesmere and across the Canterbury Plains to the Southern Alps.

The easiest descent from the hut drops down to the Kaituna Valley, a gentle track

Packhorse Hut and the mist-covered Gebbies Pass, with the Canterbury Plains and Southern Alps in the distance

taking little more than an hour, with pockets of native bush encountered on the way. Before humans arrived in this area, much of Banks Peninsula was covered with such species as totara, matai, kowhai, mahoe and fuschia. A car-swap arrangement with another party at the hut will enable you to take this different route.

Alternatively, and far more rewarding in fine weather would be to follow the track that angles up on the southern side of Mt Bradley to a low saddle and small day shelter. This is about 10 minutes below the top of Mt Herbert, with its assorted radio masts, the highest point on Banks Peninsula at 920 metres. The views from here on a clear day extend over the Lyttelton Harbour basin, with the Port Hills rising steeply on the far side, all the way to the Southern Alps stretched out along the horizon. A crisp winter's day is the best time of year to experience this fine panorama.

From the summit of Mt Herbert a couple of well-marked tracks lead down to sea level, either through Orton Bradley Park ($2 admission fee, payable at the main gate) or directly down to Diamond Harbour. Note that as there is no public transport available back up to Gebbies Pass, it is necessary to arrange a car shuttle in advance.

Winter view of Lyttelton Harbour from Mt Bradley

Cass Saddle/Lagoon Saddle

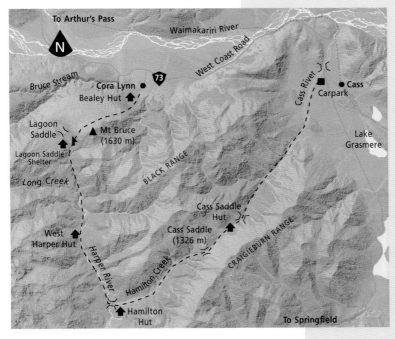

Duration: 2 days.

Grade: Moderate.

Time: 12–14 hours total. Cass River bridge (SH 73) to Cass Saddle Hut (4 bunks): 3–4 hours. Cass Saddle Hut to Hamilton Hut (20 bunks, wood stove, radio): 2 hours. Hamilton Hut to Cass River bridge via Cora Lynn Road: 6–7 hours.

Map: Wilberforce K34.

Access: Start at the Cass River bridge on SH 73, about 58 km from Springfield.

Information: DoC Arthur's Pass, Ph 03 318 9211.

WARNING! Not all rivers and streams are bridged, and can become impassable in flood conditions.

This is a fairly typical and justifiably popular weekend trip, being easily accessible from Christchurch. It is an ideal option when the weather is not so good around the Main Divide, as its easterly location often means little or no rain falls compared with the ranges further west. The route passes through a mixture of river flats, beech forests and relatively low, subalpine saddles, with regular huts. With the exception of the modern and spacious Hamilton Hut, which makes an ideal halfway point on the trail, the huts are all small two- to five-bunk shelters.

The route is fairly well signposted throughout, with regular DoC orange tree triangles and plastic warratahs above the bushline, although sections along the riverbeds allow for some individual exploration. When the weather is fine, there are excellent views during the last (or first) few hours above Bealey Hut over the broad Waimakariri Valley to the main Arthur's Pass mountains.

A large DoC signpost at the eastern end of the Cass River bridge on SH 73 points onto the stony river flats via a line of pine trees. Follow the Cass River, crossing it several times, to where the valley narrows. Carry on upstream, generally on the true right although with a few deviations to the other bank, until the track climbs into the forest to avoid the small, stony gorge section below. This is just short of the Long

Valley Stream, which flows into the main valley from the left.

Climb through this mountain beech forest, following many minor ups and downs, until the track drops to the Cass River and a bridge over to the left bank. Sidle up again, crossing some open tussock basins with occasional boardwalks over the boggy sections, to reach the small A-frame Cass Saddle Hut near the bushline. There are limited camping spots adjacent to this four-bunk hut.

Cass Saddle itself is reached after a further half-hour or so. Frequent marker poles lead across open tussocklands, interspersed with a smattering of spaniards, to a fine viewpoint overlooking Hamilton Creek and the hut far below. This section of the track receives high winter snowfalls, and at times extreme avalanche danger exists here, which is something to be aware of if you are tackling this tramp in the colder months.

The track descends steeply towards Hamilton Creek, with some small slips, then more gently through forest terraces to the valley floor. Hamilton Hut, situated on a terrace above the valley, is reached after about half an hour, the track breaking out onto grassy flats with clear views after the relative confines of the forest. Hamilton Hut is modern and spacious (20 bunks), with running water, a radio and, most importantly in the colder months, a wood stove.

Below Hamilton Hut the creek is bridged with a walkwire, a high-water alternative, which leads to a swingbridge over the Harper River a short distance above its confluence with Hamilton Creek.

Swingbridge over the West Harper

Continue upstream on the true right, with occasional forays into the forest, although it is also possible to follow the streambed in low-flow conditions. This leads to the old and classic West Harper Hut, complete with dirt floor, five canvas bunks and an open fireplace – a good option for those who eschew the frequently characterless modern huts.

A small gorge above the hut can either be bypassed above or waded across, complete with stops in summer swimming holes along the way. Stony flats lead up to a major confluence with Long Creek, crossing Harper Stream where necessary en route.

Take care here to head north up the minor valley; Long Creek, although the larger of the two tributaries, is a dead end.

Cairns mark the way up this stony riverbed and into the forest on the true left, which, after the usual up and downs, arrives at Lagoon Saddle Shelter. This is a small A-frame (two bunks, wood stove) built in a clearing; another 'garden-shed' hut (three bunks) is sited slightly higher, across the river (both are four to five hours from Hamilton Hut).

A short section of forest leads out onto the tops above the tarn on Lagoon Saddle, from where the view northwards opens up dramatically. Far below flows the braided Waimakariri, while the snow-topped peaks around Arthur's Pass dominate the skyline on a clear day.

Skirt around the shoulder of Mt Bruce, where sections of the frequently boggy track are being boardwalked, before dropping down to where the path enters a mixed beech/exotic forest. Finally, zigzag some 400 metres down through this forest to the six-bunk Bealey Hut and Cora Lynn Road, passing the Wilderness Lodge just before the main highway. All that follows for those without prior pickup arrangements is an 11-kilometre jog or cycle ride back to the Cass River bridge.

Down towards Bealey Hut, with the Waimakariri River below

Tarn Col/Walker Pass

Duration: 2–3 days.

Grade: Hard.

Time: 18 hours total. SH 73 to
Edwards Hut: 5 hours. Edwards
Hut (14 bunks) to East Otehake
River: 6 hours. East Otehake River
to Hawdon Shelter: 7 hours.

Maps: Otira K33, Arthur's Pass
Parkmap 273/01.

Access: SH 73 to the layby 6 km
south of Arthur's Pass village.

Alternative Routes: There are
many options once you are in
Edwards Valley, in particular the
climb over the north shoulder
of Mt Oates and descent to Goat
Pass via Lake Mavis.

Information: DoC Arthur's Pass,
Ph 03 318 9211.

WARNING! The Bealey and
Hawdon rivers can both become
impassable during heavy rain.

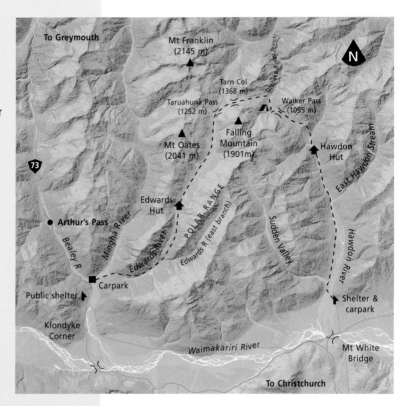

This classic tramp in Arthur's Pass National Park
encompasses all that is good about heading off
into the hills for a long weekend. The route takes you from beech forests to subalpine
river flats, across two mountain passes complete with picturesque tarns, over the Main
Divide for a night among West Coast bush and then back down to a broad, open river
valley. Between the two DoC huts the route is either unmarked, or marked only with
the occasional rock cairn or pole. There are no bridges and the rivers and streams
require frequent crossings, so this is a wet-boot trip and one that can only safely be
undertaken in dry, low-water conditions. For trampers unaccustomed to this type of
travel, times may be longer than those indicated, as is the case if the route is followed
in reverse.

Start six kilometres south of Arthur's Pass village at a large layby next to the
railtrack. There is a DoC sign and an intentions book here. Wade the Bealey River
just above its confluence with the Mingha; if you have problems here with high water,
remember that there are many more rivers to cross on this trip and you may therefore
want to consider abandoning it until conditions are drier.

Cut across the valley, fording the Mingha en route, to where large and obvious DoC orange triangles mark the entrance into the beech forest, below the junction of the Edwards River. This bypasses the lower Edwards Gorge, which is a fun alternative if the water levels are sufficiently low. The track re-emerges onto the river flats, which are followed on the true left bank (with occasional diversions into the forest) until you reach the east branch of the Edwards. The track crosses this river – difficult in high flow – above its junction with the main valley, to pick up a marked track some 100 metres upstream leading back into the forest. This is about the halfway point to the hut.

From here the track climbs steeply up the forested valley sides, an ascent often on tree-root and rock 'stairways', to avoid the waterfalls that tumble down the deep gorge of the Edwards River below. Eventually, the track emerges onto tussocklands at the bushline. The spacious 14-bunk Edwards Hut is a welcome sight in the distance, some 20 minutes further on.

From Edwards Hut, follow the true left bank of the river up towards Taruahuna Pass. Stick mainly to a track through the tussocks, although at times you may find it preferable to cross to the right bank, thereby avoiding small sections of scrub-bashing in favour of the stony riverbed. Look out for blue ducks in the main river as you go, listening for the characteristic whistle of the male. These ducks are the only native

Upper Hawdon Valley from below Walker Pass

species to inhabit fast-flowing mountain streams, and their whitewater antics are well worth watching if you are lucky enough to spot them in the Edwards River.

The head of the valley is dominated by a huge pile of rock debris, the result of the 1929 earthquake (6.9 on the Richter scale) that not only damaged Arthur's Pass village but also shook off a sizeable part of Falling Mountain. This vast rockslide now smothers Taruahuna Pass, over which an indistinct track weaves its way to the high point of the saddle before turning abruptly northeast and climbing up to the obvious low point in the range on the right. Tarn Col is best approached from this side by ascending directly along the streambed that drains from the lowest point of the col, bypassing the small waterfall on the true left by a steep snowgrass slope. Great care should be taken here, especially in wet or icy conditions, as a slip could be fatal. (If you are travelling east to west, it is possible to avoid this steep snowgrass by descending the scree slope at the southern end of the col, a preferable route down into the Edwards Valley.) The climb to the small lake nestled among boulders and tussock on the top of Tarn Col takes about 45 minutes from Taruahuna Pass.

Alpine tarn on Walker Pass

Enjoy the views from this high point – the steep flanks of Mt Franklin dominate the scenery to the northwest, while the peaks to the east lie within the Otehake Wilderness Area. If you plan to camp in the main valley below, linger here and enjoy the solitude, as the night's camp is about two hours away.

After crossing the flat tussock country nestled in the saddle for about five minutes, drop into a creek that drains from the tarn above. Resist staying above this steep little gorge, as bluffs soon prevent further travel on the top. This creek is followed, and crossed many times, before you join the east branch of the Otehake River, from where the track crosses to the true right bank and heads upstream to a delightful little campsite on the river flats. You are now on the western side of the Main Divide, noticeable by the presence of mountain neinei, leatherwood and tree daisy among the scrub that grows thickly on the hillsides.

From the riverside camp, continue upvalley for about 20 minutes to where the river swings to the right (southwest) towards Amber Col. A cairned track leads up left into scrub, and is followed to the low saddle known as Walker Pass. This also has a small tarn in its basin, and once again the route follows the outlet creek draining through dense subalpine scrub. A track zigzags along this creek, and although it requires care to follow, it is a more pleasant prospect than battling through the dense dracophyllum scrub on the valley sides. Marker poles show where the track leaves the creek and climbs steeply up to a rocky knob, with a fine view both up to Walker Pass and down to the broad meanders of the Hawdon River, some 300 metres below.

Pick up a good, though steep, track that descends through beech forest and past the Twin Falls to the valley floor below. The well-marked track continues at a far more gentle angle to reach the Hawdon Hut (16 bunks) after about 20 more minutes.

The broad Hawdon River valley is now followed down to the roadend, about three hours from the hut. Take the track on the true right until the east branch of the river flows in from the left; it is then easier to cross the river and continue on the grassy flats until you near Sudden Valley Stream.

A more verdant alternative to the open flats in the middle of the valley involves recrossing the main river to pick up an old 4WD track that skirts the bush edge, where you have small tributary streams for company. Cross the river just downstream of the farm fence and enter the forest for a gentle sidle up to the Hawdon Shelter and the roadend. As the end point of this tramp is 22 kilometres via road to the start, you will need to arrange in advance for a car or bicycle to be left for you so that you can drive or cycle over the Mt White Bridge to the main highway.

Tramper on Walker Pass

Avalanche Peak/Crow Valley   ARTHUR'S PASS NATIONAL PARK

Duration: 2 days.

Grade: Moderate.

Time: 9–12 hours total. Arthur's Pass village to Avalanche Peak: 3–4 hours. Avalanche Peak to Crow Hut (10 bunks, wood stove): 3 hours. Crow Hut to Waimakariri Flats: 2–3 hours. Waimakariri Flats to Klondyke Corner: 1–2 hours.

Maps: Otira K33, Wilberforce K34.

Access: From Arthur's Pass village.

Alternative Routes: Avalanche Peak as can be climbed as a day trip from Arthur's Pass village. This tramp can also be combined with the next walk (see page 108), to Waimakariri Falls Hut.

Information: DoC Arthur's Pass, Ph 03 318 9211.

WARNING! This is an alpine area. Snow and ice on the tops could make the trip dangerous, and the risk of avalanche is high at certain times of the year. The route is also subject to river levels, as there are no bridges along the way.

This is a very popular trip, especially since a new hut in the Crow Valley was built to replace the much older and tattier version. The tramp over Avalanche Peak into the Crow Valley and down to the Waimakariri and Klondyke Corner can be enjoyed in a leisurely two days, or alternatively run in as little as four hours if you plan on participating in the Avalanche Peak Challenge. Good weather is required for the climb over the 1833-metre-high peak itself, and since the views from there are one of the main attractions of this tramp it would be prudent to wait for a clear day.

There are two tracks leading up from the village to the summit of Avalanche Peak: the slightly gentler Scotts Track and the more direct Avalanche Creek Track, both of which are well marked throughout. Either way, there are over 1000 metres to ascend, so be prepared for a steep and, on hot days, a sweaty climb.

The more direct track starts just up from the DoC visitor centre in Arthur's Pass village and before a bridge over the creek. It clambers straight up through a forest of mountain beech, the exposed roots of which are put to good use as convenient handholds on the steeper sections. There are some attractive waterfalls down in the creekbed, but as these are not easy to access you should remember to take enough to drink for the waterless ascent over to the Crow Valley.

The bushline is reached after an hour or so, from where a tussock spur leads at a slightly gentler angle towards the peak. There are frequent yellow poles along this section (with a different colour code for Scotts Track, which comes in from the north and joins up with this track about 15 minutes below the top); these should always be followed, since either side of the exposed ridge there are some serious drop-offs and impassable bluffs. Particular care should be taken when snow is lying on the upper slopes of the mountain – often the case well into summer.

It takes between three and four hours for the climb to the top and, weather permitting, an excellent lunch stop on the shale summit of Avalanche Peak should be included. The uninterrupted views along the ridge to Mt Rolleston and the Crow Glacier are superb, this ridge being the route taken before dropping down to the Crow Valley.

En route to Crow Valley from Mt Avalanche, with Mt Rolleston beyond

Crow Hut and Mt Rolleston, Arthur's Pass National Park

There are no direct routes down into the Crow Valley from the top of Avalanche Peak, as the slope leads to dangerous bluffs. Instead, drop down to the south side of the peak (this is the opposite direction to the eventual route taken) and skirt around the summit on scree to gain the ridge running northwards towards Mt Rolleston. This is followed on more scree slopes to the eastern, or village, side of the ridge until you reach a distinct rise ahead, at which point marker posts show the way down to the Crow Valley. It is important to locate the correct descent route to avoid being bluffed out; a reliable indicator in clear visibility is when the entire drop of the Punchbowl Falls across the valley can first be seen.

A rough and blocky scree slope leads directly down to the valley floor (note that this is a potential avalanche risk area in heavy snow). The Crow Hut can be seen from near the bottom of this scree slope on the true right of the Crow River. To reach the hut, follow the river downstream for half an hour, crossing as soon as possible if the water is running high. Opened in May 2002, Crow Hut has 10 berths and a wood stove, This valley gets its name from a sighting, in 1865, of the South Island kokako, or orange-wattled crow, last seen in the Arthur's Pass area in the 1930s and nowadays presumed extinct.

In springtime, the grassy flats around here are dotted with luscious clusters of the Mount Cook 'lily', a common misnomer for the world's largest buttercup, *Ranunculus lyallii*. Found only in the South Island mountains, this most splendid of alpine plants provides an added dimension to early summer tramps, and is usually in full bloom from November and into December, depending on aspect, altitude and latitude.

There are good views of the South Face of Mt Rolleston, at the head of the Crow Valley, from the Crow Hut door. As the second day of this trip involves a leisurely four-hour stroll downvalley to Klondyke Corner, stay awhile and enjoy the peace of this spot; read a book or take an icy morning dip in the river.

The track down from the hut follows the true right bank of the cascading Crow River, alternating between grassy flats and beech forest. Some two hours of easy travel leads to where the river begins to flow out across shingle flats in the main valley, at which point it can usually be crossed without problem. From here, cut through a small patch of forest to the Waimakariri Flats.

The grassy or shingle banks of the Waimakariri River are followed on its north side, although at one stage bluffs force you to cross and recross the river, before you pick up the rough vehicle track leading to Klondyke Corner on SH 73. Arthur's Pass village is about eight kilometres along the road from here.

Mount Cook buttercup, Arthur's Pass National Park

Waimakariri Falls/Mt Philistine ARTHUR'S PASS NATIONAL PARK

Duration: 2 days.

Grade: Moderate/easy mountaineering.

Time: 16–18 hours total. Klondyke Corner to Carrington Hut (36 bunks): 4–5 hours. Carrington Hut to Waimakariri Falls Hut (6 bunks): 3 hours. Waimakariri Falls Hut to Waimakariri Col: 2 hours. Waimakariri Col to SH 73 via Mt Philistine: 7–8 hours.

Maps: Otira K33, Wilberforce K34.

Access: Klondyke Corner, on SH 73, located 8 km south of Arthur's Pass village.

Alternative Routes: Descend all the way down Rolleston Valley from the saddle by Waimakariri Col (allow 8–10 hours to reach SH 73).

Information: DoC Arthur's Pass, Ph 03 318 9211.

WARNING! Unbridged rivers. Snow is likely to be encountered for much of the year, and crampons and ice axe are necessary pieces of equipment.

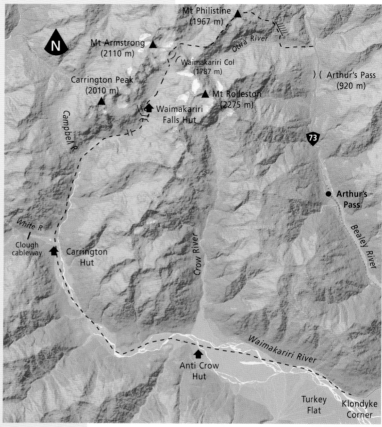

A trip across the Main Divide over Waimakariri Col is one of those must-do tramps on many people's checklist. The gravel slog up the 'Waimak' perhaps puts some parties off this weekend excursion, but it shouldn't, as the terrain is varied and interesting, and there is a very special little hut in which to spend a cosy night. If combined with an ascent of Mt Philistine on the second day, this tramp does require experience with crampons and ice axes. However, if you do not have these skills you can descend the Rolleston River instead to reach the main highway north of Arthur's Pass, although this tramp would merit a 'hard' grade.

The track starts at Klondyke Corner, on SH 73, just beyond the long road bridge over the Waimakariri River, where there is a carpark and rough section of road leading down to the river gravels. The route upvalley will vary depending on the state of the river, but always involves a few crossings back and forth to avoid sections of bluffs along the true left. There is a flood track on the opposite side of the valley, starting adjacent to the long road bridge and following a benched track up the true right until it drops down to Turkey Flat and beyond. However, if river levels warrant this approach then you should consider altering your plans, since there are a number of quite difficult side creeks that need to be crossed before you reach Carrington Hut.

Although the terrain underfoot can appear monotonous, take time to appreciate the mosses, cushion plants and small shrubs that survive out on these often windswept river flats. The grander picture, however, is always dramatic, with peaks rising up on both sides of the valley. Rich green forests decorate their lower slopes and huge scree slides smother the upper reaches of these typical Arthur's Pass mountains.

The walk to the large Carrington Hut (36 bunks, radio) takes most parties between four and five hours. If you are linking this trip up with the Mt Avalanche and Crow Valley tramp (see page 104), allow three hours to reach the hut from the bottom of the Crow Valley. Carrington Hut makes an ideal base for day trips to a number of destinations: up the White River to Barker Hut, below Mt Murchison; up to Harman Pass, which leads over to the Taipo River; or to Waimakariri Col and back. From Carrington Hut it takes a further three to four hours to reach the much more intimate Waimakariri Falls Hut; staying here puts you in a suitable position to complete the trip in the allotted two days.

The glacially fed White River is crossed soon after you leave the hut (if it is running high you can use the cableway 20 minutes upstream). There is an intermittently marked track on the true right of this upper section of the Waimakariri River, passing through sections of forest and along the riverbank, with views upvalley to the rugged

Waimakariri Falls Hut and Waimakariri Col

Carrington Peak. After an hour it opens out into subalpine scrub and herbfields, with the Campbell River flowing in from the west. Beyond this junction the main river takes a sweep to the east; it is easier to cut this corner by crossing the river, thereby avoiding the outside bend and small bluffs above.

The valley becomes narrower and more impressive as the Waimakariri Falls are approached. Here, water-falls cascade over the crags and chasms above, and a varied array of alpine flowers studs the hillsides: Mount Cook buttercups (*Ranunculus lyallii*), mountain foxgloves (*Ourisia macrocarpa*), delicate eyebrights (*Euphrasia revoluta*), papery everlasting daisies (*Helichrysum bellidioides*) and many more to delight the amateur botanist during the summer months.

On the ridge of Mt Philistine looking to Mt Rolleston

Shortly before you reach the as yet invisible falls, and just before the start of the main gorge, the track again crosses to the true right. Initially the route is very steep as it climbs away from the riverbed through scrub to reach, after about five minutes, a fine viewpoint overlooking the thundering waterfalls below. Higher up, be on the lookout for cairns along a tussocky, boulder-strewn terrace above the gorge, especially when crossing a rocky side stream.

A section of large boulders has to be negotiated just before a tricky descent to a swingbridge over the chasm, with the sound of crashing waterfalls above. From here, a 10-minute climb leads to the more open upper valley, passing some tarns before reaching the small orange shed of the Waimakariri Falls Hut (six bunks), perched above a rocky cleft.

The area around this cosy little hut is worth exploring. The stream above is fringed with clusters of buttercups in November and December, and a cautious scramble above the gloomy depths of the chasm directly downstream reveals the erosive power of water as it plunges 80 metres over this fault lip. Back down the valley, Mt Murchison (at 2408 metres the highest peak in the park) dominates the southern skyline, while the route up to Waimakariri Col is clearly obvious upvalley.

This can be quite a long day whichever route is taken for the descent, so consider rising early and watching the sunrise on the glacier fields of Mt Murchison, thereby making the most of the available time. The route towards the Waimakariri Col is initially quite clear as it follows the true left side of the stream until it flows out of a small ravine in the bottom of the valley. Cross over just below here to the true right, and scramble up scree or snow slopes through a line of bluffs to the crest of the broad saddle above.

The actual Waimakariri Col does not lead down easily to the Rolleston River on its northern side; the better crossing point is reached by heading in a northwesterly direction around Pt 1845 until you are directly below the Mt Armstrong Glacier.

Easy snow slopes usually lead down from the saddle, but be careful early in the morning as the surface may be frozen. Because snow covers much of these upper sections of the route, it is important to carry crampons and ice axes, especially for the climb over Mt Philistine.

It is necessary to drop down a considerable distance from the saddle, before a straightforward slope of snow or, later in the season, scree leads back across to the high ridge that connects Mt Rolleston with Mt Philistine. Do not be tempted to head directly to this ridge from the saddle, as lines of steep bluffs bar the way.

Choose the best line up to the ridge depending on conditions, gaining it somewhere near Pt 1860. Travel northwards along the ridge is quite easy, whereas the way south to Mt Rolleston should only be attempted by experienced parties. The Philistine–Rolleston Ridge is a spectacular place to be on a clear summer's morning, but should be avoided in bad weather or poor visibility. Allow four hours from the hut to this point if conditions are good and firm, but longer in soft snow. It takes an hour or so along this delightfully airy ridgetop to reach the large bulk of 1967-metre Mt Philistine, which dominates the view northwards. The final section involves some straightforward scrambling on the western side to the panoramic summit.

The best descent will depend on the season, but a smooth snow slope normally leads down a short distance north of the summit directly to a broad basin below, thereby avoiding the steeper and sharper East Ridge. From this basin, follow the gently dropping broad ridge to a point above the Philistine Bluffs. The route through this short but steep line of cliffs is cairned and well trodden, but is an unforgiving place in which to lose your footing – there have been accidents here.

Once below these bluffs, the track drops off the ridge leading to Warnock's Knob, and heads down tussocks and scree to the Otira River and the main footpath along the valley floor. Reach this at the wooden footbridge, where there is an icy pool for an afternoon dip before the final half-hour's stroll to the highway. Arthur's Pass village is about six kilometres down the road, and it is usually possible to hitch a ride from here.

Mingha/Deception
ARTHUR'S PASS NATIONAL PARK

Duration: 2 days.

Grade: Moderate.

Time: 11 hours total. Otira River footbridge (SH 73) to Goat Pass Hut (20 bunks): 6 hours. Goat Pass Hut to Bealey River and SH 73: 5 hours.

Map: Otira K33.

Access: From SH 73 in the Otira Valley, 20 km north of Arthur's Pass and 3 km north of Kelly Creek day shelter.

Information: DoC Arthur's Pass, Ph 03 318 9211.

WARNING! As is the case throughout this alpine area, the rivers can become impassable during heavy rain.

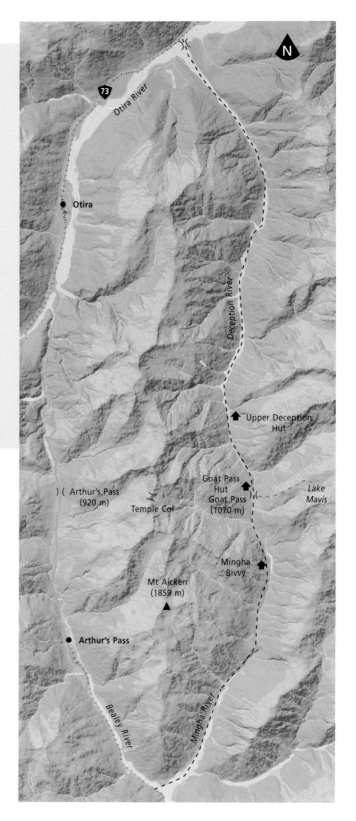

Lake Mavis, Arthur's Pass National Park

This two-day trip across the Main Divide of the Southern Alps offers a good weekend tramp for people based in Christchurch. The route forms the mountain-run section of the annual Coast to Coast competition, and although it is frequently completed in less than three hours during the race, most weekend trampers will prefer the more leisurely option described below. In good conditions, the tramp presents no problems, but be aware that some sections – particularly in the Deception Valley – are rough and the track is not regularly marked. Allow time to make the worthwhile side trip up to Lake Mavis from Goat Pass Hut, all the more enjoyable without a heavy pack.

A few kilometres north of the Kelly Creek day shelter on SH 73, a substantial foot-bridge crosses the Otira River to the bottom of the Deception Valley. The advantage of walking this route from north to south is that you can tell how high the river is right at the start – if it is running too high here, then conditions will be even more difficult further up. If this if the case, save the tramp for another day and go up to Carroll Hut instead.

The Deception River, originally known as Goat River, was renamed by a surveyor for the railway company who warned that the volume of water this river could carry in flood was deceptive. His warnings proved prophetic when, a few months later, a major flood carried away a lot of expensive railway works downstream.

Beyond the initial shingle flats, cross the Deception River to the true left bank and continue into the lower gorge. Although this is not a marked track as such, there are a number of small cairns along the way, presumably erected to aid the Coast to Coast runners when they come through each February. There are occasional deviations into the forest, but by and large the route follows the bouldery riverbed closely, crossing whenever necessary. Pass a now defunct footbridge leading to the true right and continue upstream, weaving in and out of typically large, West Coast boulders, sparing a thought for those among us who run over such terrain.

Crossing a swollen side stream on the Mingha River

The Upper Deception Hut (six bunks), passed after about five hours, is sited on the true right just after Good Luck Creek. Continue for a further hour up the riverbed, or follow vague tracks through nearby bush, which lead to a final scramble up a small side creek with a pole marking this junction. The spacious Goat Pass Hut (20 bunks and a radio) is situated in subalpine scrub just short of the pass itself. Note that the old wood stove has been removed for safety and environmental reasons, and as the hut is at an altitude of over 1000 metres it can get pretty cold.

In good weather it is well worth getting up early to include a three- to four-hour side trip to the beautifully situated Lake Mavis, tucked below the gloomy precipices of Mt Oates. Leaving your pack at the hut, ascend tussock and scree slopes east of the pass to a distinct ridge leading up to the lake (allow two hours for the climb up). In late summer the shores of this alpine lake are ringed with daisies (*Senecio* spp.).

Back at Goat Pass Hut, extensive sections of boardwalk cross the fragile upland bogs leading to the Upper Mingha Valley. Stop to observe the mosses and insectivorous sundews that inhabit these wetlands.

Unlike the track along the Deception Valley, that down the Mingha is well marked and easy to follow in most conditions. Subalpine scrub soon gives way to open beech forest, and you pass the old and dilapidated Mingha Bivvy (two bunks) in a clearing before you reach the bushline. Keeping well above the impassable gorge below, climb the gentle slope to Dudley's Knob, where there are views of the surrounding mountains. This is a good picnic place on a sunny day before you tackle the final hour or so down to the valley flats of the Lower Mingha.

The Bealey River is forded near its confluence with the Mingha – check for the best spot as this will change from time to time. It is only five minutes to the road from here, but if it has been raining and the rivers are running high then stay put or return to Mingha Bivvy. Accidents have happened here when impatient weekenders have attempted to cross in dangerous conditions.

Lake Mavis, Arthur's Pass National Park

Mt Somers Walkway

Duration: 2–3 days.

Grade: Moderate.

Time: 10 hours total. Sharplin Falls carpark to Pinnacles Hut (18 bunks, wood stove): 4 hours. Pinnacles Hut to Mt Somers Hut (18 bunks, wood stove): 3.5 hours. Mt Somers Hut to roadend via Trig R: 2 hours. Mt Somers Hut to roadend via Woolshed Creek Canyon: 4 hours.

Map: Methven K36.

Access: Turn off the Geraldine–Darfield road (SH 72) 5 km north of Mt Somers village and 10 km south of Mt Hutt skifield entrance, following signs to Staveley. The route starts at the Sharplin Falls carpark.

Alternative Routes: It is possible to climb the long but gentle Northwest Ridge to the summit of Mt Somers (1687 m) from near the junction of Woolshed Creek and Morgan Stream (allow 3 hours). An alternative return route follows Woolshed Creek Canyon.

Information: DoC Geraldine, Ph 03 693 9994. The Mt Somers Walkway Society is in the process of linking up either end of the walkway to create a loop track around the mountain. This will extend the time required for the tramp, but will negate the present transport arrangement problems. A shuttle back to Sharplin Falls carpark from the roadend can be arranged in advance through Mt Somers village store, Ph 03 303 9831. The Mt Somers Hut is owned by the Mt Somers Walkway Society but administered by DoC. Annual hut passes are not valid for this hut; instead, tickets can be purchased from Mt Somers or Staveley stores.

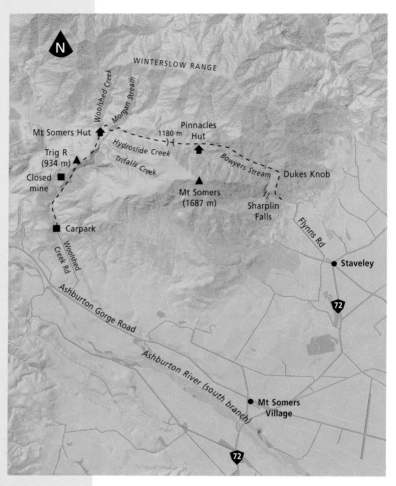

Mt Somers is the prominent conical-shaped peak immediately to the south of Mt Hutt, and as it is only one-and-a-half hours' drive from Christchurch it is a popular weekend destination for trampers heading to the hills. The excellent Mt Somers Walkway was developed by a dedicated group of locals in the late 1980s as a tramping route around the northern side of this isolated volcanic outlier, and provides access to some varied landscapes. The route travels from beech and broadleaf forests up to the subalpine scrub and tussock uplands, passing through some impressive rock scenery, including towering columnar jointed cliffs, strange pinnacles and deep canyons. If you allow yourself an extra day or two, there are plenty of opportunities for exploring the area more fully.

Start at the Sharplin Falls carpark (470 metres), where there is an information board, an intentions book and toilets. It is always a good idea to fill in the intentions book at trailheads, both for safety and for an indication of the numbers of people you can expect along the trail. From here, the track crosses a bridge over the Bowyers Stream and then climbs steeply for half an hour to Dukes Knob (740 metres), before dropping back down to the streambed. Boulder-hop along the stream and cross it a few times before climbing out onto a spur on the true right.

In springtime, the lower sections of the beech forest you pass through on this section are adorned with creamy-white clusters of the climbing native clematis *(Clematis paniculata)*, providing a welcome splash of colour among the greenery. The dominant trees here are black and mountain beech, along with broadleaf, marbleleaf and the characteristic lancewood growing in the understorey. The beech trees usually have a distinctive sooty black trunk, which is a fungal growth that harbours an insect important to the ecology of the forest. The parasitic scale insect *(Ultracoelostoma assimile)* concealed within the fungus takes more sugars from the tree than it is capable of processing, and the excess is secreted to the outside via a thin white tube. This 'honeydew' is a major food source for the nectar-feeders of the forest, in particular bellbirds, tui, kaka and silvereyes. Unfortunately, it is also much sought after by introduced wasps, which compete aggressively with native species – the latter are declining as a consequence. In late summer, the wasp population of these beech forests peaks; the background hum at this time is ever-present and care should be taken when using

From near Pinnacles Hut

honeydew-draped tree trunks as handholds.

The well-marked track eventually reaches the bushline and the more open uplands of the subalpine area. Much of the walkway passes through this exposed high country, and caution is recommended in adverse weather as the route climbs to nearly 1200 metres on the second day.

Columnar jointed rhyolite bluffs, Mt Somers

The modern, comfortable Pinnacles Hut comes into view at the crest of a small saddle, and is reached after crossing two small streams. It is named after the andesite pinnacles that lie scattered over the hillside here. Along with the huge columns of rhyolite higher up the mountainside, these pinnacles are geological evidence that the Mt Somers region has a volcanic origin, unlike much of the Southern Alps foothills in this area. The cliffs are becoming a popular playground for rock climbers, who often spend a few days at the hut in order to explore them fully.

The scene from the Pinnacles Hut, framed by the forested valley sides of Bowyers Stream, stretches across the green patchwork of the Canterbury Plains to the hills of Banks Peninsula, another volcanic outlier. For much of the summer the sun rises directly behind these coastal hills to shine directly into the hut, guaranteeing an early start for the walk through to Mt Somers hut and, if time is limited, to the end of the track.

A steady climb of about one-and-a-half hours through tussock country dotted with numerous species of summer-flowering mountain daisies (*Celmisia* spp.) brings you to the 1170-metre saddle that forms the watershed between Bowyers Stream and Woolshed Creek. The broad track continues downvalley, skirting the northern flanks of 1687-metre-high Mt Somers itself. The main trail then crosses Morgan Stream, the crags above which are a frequent haunt of the New Zealand falcon, and climbs over an intervening spur before dropping down to the main Woolshed Creek. Mt Somers Hut is sited by this creek, a characterful old musterers' hut with two rooms and 18 bunks. It has a wood stove and there is a small log-cabin sauna five minutes upstream. There are plans to build a new hut at this site in the not-too-distant future.

The Woolshed Creek area has plenty of watery attractions if time allows. An extra day spent exploring the Water Caves, Hydroslide and Trifalls Creek, as well as soaking away any aches in the nearby 'bush sauna' after a refreshing pummelling under the Spa Pool waterfall (downstream from the hut), is well worth including in the trip.

It is possible to walk out to the roadend in two hours from here, climbing away from the impassible upper canyon of Woolshed Creek to Trig R (934 metres). This is a fine viewpoint overlooking the extensive glaciated landscape stretching westwards to the Arrowsmith Range and the Southern Alps. From this high point, drop steadily downhill, following a poled route across tussock basins to the now defunct Blackburn coal mine. This mine finally closed in the 1960s after many years of intermittent activity; there are still remnants of the industry scattered around the hillside, including the old jig railway and a hopper lying wrecked at the bottom of the steep incline. The track zigzags steeply down to the forested valley floor and reaches the carpark after a further 20 minutes.

An alternative route out takes the signed track just before Trig R, descending steeply to the beautifully enclosed Woolshed Creek Canyon below. In normal flow this can be followed all the way to the carpark, thereby offering an entertaining 'off-route' trail. This involves boulder-hopping and wading the many crystal-clear pools, with a few divergences into the beech forest on either side to avoid the deeper pools and small waterfalls. There are plenty of opportunities for a swim along the way, but despite the fact that it is not far in distance, this section is time-consuming – allow four hours from the hut to the roadend via this route. It is not recommended in high-water flows.

The Canterbury Plains and Banks Peninsula, seen from Mt Somers

Mueller Hut/Mt Ollivier

AORAKI/MOUNT COOK NATIONAL PARK

Duration: 2 days.

Grade: Moderate.

Time: 7 hours total. Aoraki/
Mount Cook village to Mueller
Hut (30 bunks, gas heating): 4
hours. Mueller Hut to Aoraki/
Mount Cook village: 3 hours.

Maps: Mount Cook H36, Aoraki/
Mount Cook Alpine Area special
map.

Access: Start at Aoraki/Mount
Cook village, or drive out to
White Horse Hill campground.

Information: DoC Aoraki/Mount
Cook, Ph 03 435 1818.

WARNING! In winter and spring
snow and ice can often be
encountered en route to the hut,
requiring the use of an ice axe
and crampons. At certain times
of the year there can be a high
avalanche risk on the upper sections of the route, so
always check conditions at the park visitor centre
before you set out.

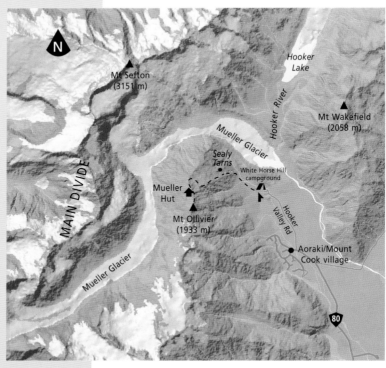

Aoraki/Mount Cook National Park has some of
the most spectacular alpine scenery anywhere
in New Zealand, but since much of it is heavily
glaciated, large tracts are accessible only to those
with alpine experience and a good knowledge of glacier travel. However, a summer trip
to Mueller Hut, at 1800 metres, allows the averagely fit tramper to access the heart of
these majestic mountains without the need for any specialised knowledge or equipment.

Either start at the village or drive to White Horse Hill carpark, from where a good
track leads gently through subalpine scrub toward Kea Point and the turnoff for Sealy
Tarns. The climb up to Sealy Tarns and the Mueller Range is marked by an orange
triangle at this turnoff and abruptly becomes a lot steeper. The track is well marked,
and after about two hours of zigzagging up the hillside you emerge on a narrow terrace
with small mountain lakes nestled in the dip. These are the Sealy Tarns, which on a
hot day offer great swimming with views of the adjacent icefalls and the classic form
of Aoraki/Mt Cook dominating the view northwards. The alpine tussock surrounding
these waterholes is home, in springtime, to great clusters of Mount Cook buttercups

(Ranunculus lyallii), replaced later in the season by large mountain daisies (*Celmisia* spp.) and lastly by the autumnal gentians (*Gentiana* spp.).

The extent to which the glaciers in this area have receded in recent history is quite apparent as you gaze across the remains of the Lower Mueller Glacier to the steep, but now ice-free, moraine wall and into the Hooker Valley. Here, the lateral, or side, moraines pick out an earlier level of this once-mighty river of ice, now reduced to a shrunken and melting glacier with an ever-enlarging lake below its terminal face.

Aoraki/Mt Cook from Sealy Tarns

Above the tarns the route is not a formed track, although it is sufficiently well trodden to be quite obvious. Occasional orange markers and cairns show the way as it zigzags through tussockland and across a large boulder field to a final steep scramble up scree to the ridgetop on the skyline. The view from here justifies the exertion, as the huge East Face of Mt Sefton rises from the Mueller Glacier directly below, draped in hanging glaciers that frequently send cataracts of ice crashing down to feed the great frozen river at their feet.

Turn south from here along the ridge and weave between large orange-hued sandstone boulders to reach the Mueller Hut in about 15 minutes. This 30-bed hut was built in the autumn of 2003 to replace the classic, but rather tatty, earlier hut that for 50 years had withstood the winter storms that regularly sweep over this exposed ridge, 1800 metres above sea-level. The new hut has a radio, gas heating and solar lighting, but note that it is not covered by hut passes and is priced at a higher level. A night spent in the shelter of such a sturdy refuge while a storm rages unabated outside is not to be forgotten. In the summer months a warden is often in residence, and as this is one of the few areas in the region accessible to non-mountaineers, the hut becomes quite crowded; limited camping spots are available nearby.

Mt Ollivier (1933 metres) offers an even better viewpoint than the hut itself, and the chance to bag what was supposedly Sir Edmund Hillary's first alpine peak in the South Island. This summit, marked by a large cairn, is reached via a rocky scramble along the ridge from the hut in about 30 minutes. Avoid the temptation to continue further as the ridge soon becomes steep and loose.

On the return, follow the same route as for the ascent, taking particular care in poor visibility to locate correctly the ill-defined trail leading from the ridgetop down the scree slope below. There is often a snow patch here; if so, be aware that what was soft and straightforward yesterday afternoon could well have become a solid, icy slope after a cold night. There have been a number of accidents over the years on this slope, usually the result of inexperience with snow conditions. If you are in doubt, it is better to wait until later in the day when the snow has begun to soften.

Finally, when you are back down, remember to report your return after an overnight trip at the park headquarters, and to pay any outstanding hut fees.

Mount Cook buttercups above Sealy Tarns, Aoraki/Mount Cook National Park

Ball Pass

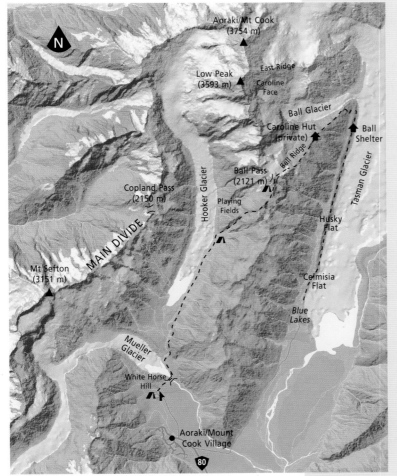

Duration: 2 days.

Grade: Moderate to hard (mountaineering and route-finding skills required).

Time: 12–13 hours total. Celmisia Flat to Ball Shelter (sleeping benches for 8): 2 hours. Ball Shelter to Ball Pass: 5 hours. Ball Pass to valley floor: 3 hours. Valley floor to White Horse Hill campground: 2–3 hours.

Maps: Mount Cook H36, Aoraki/Mount Cook Alpine Area special map.

Access: Start at Blue Lakes or Celmisia Flat carpark; 4WD vehicles can go on to Husky Flat.

Information: DoC Aoraki/Mount Cook, Ph 03 435 1818. Alpine Recreation Canterbury runs two- or three-day guided trips over the pass, Ph 03 680 6736.

WARNING! This is a true alpine crossing, reaching an altitude of over 2000 metres and requiring route-finding knowledge. Expect to encounter snow and ice throughout the year – crampons and an ice axe are essential, plus the skills to use them. The best time for the trip is December–March.

Ball Pass is a challenging high-alpine crossing, with spectacular views to Aoraki/Mt Cook, across to the Main Divide peaks of Mt Sefton and The Footstool, and down onto the Hooker and Tasman glaciers. In the last 10 years this historically significant alpine crossing has gained popularity, largely due to the fact that the route over the Copland Pass to the west has become increasingly problematic due to severe erosion caused by glacial recession. In addition, a private guiding company (Alpine Recreation Canterbury) has set up a commercial venture, based at the purpose-built Caroline Hut, taking trampers over Ball Pass. This has helped to raise the profile of this excellent trip in the Aoraki/Mount Cook National Park. A definite advantage this tramp has over the Copland Pass route is that it lies entirely within the park, therefore avoiding the transport arrangements required for any crossing of the Main Divide to the West Coast.

Ball Pass crosses the Aoraki/Mt Cook Range at an altitude of 2121 metres, linking up the Hooker Valley with the Tasman Valley. It can be tackled from either side, the choice depending largely on personal preference; in this account, an east–west crossing is described, with a camp high on the Ball Pass for the adventurous. The alternative

approach, from a low camp up the East Hooker Valley, would be preferable if the weather or conditions are not perfect, but expect the ascent to Ball Pass from this side to take longer.

The regularly maintained road up the Tasman Valley finishes at Blue Lakes carpark, although most vehicles can get over the rough shingle fan to Celmisia Flat. Beyond here the going is suitable only for 4WDs which can make it as far as Husky Flat.

From Husky Flat the track along the old, slumped Ball Road leads high up above the moraine wastelands of the Lower Tasman

Mount Cook buttercups on Ball Ridge with Tasman Glacier below

Glacier, nowadays a mere shadow of its former self. Two hours of easy walking (note that there is no water along this stretch) takes you to the small Ball Shelter, situated on a grassy terrace close to the moraine wall. It has sleeping benches for eight, plus a supply of water, a toilet and a radio. It is possible to make a day trip to Ball Pass from this shelter – allow at least 10 hours to complete the return trip comfortably.

From the shelter, follow the worn trail along a high terrace towards the bottom of Ball Ridge. A cairn is located among the subalpine scrub before you reach the rather rotten base of this ridge. The track heads abruptly uphill from here, weaving between some large boulders and loose scree slides, to where the angle eases off. In springtime these slopes are adorned with magnificent clusters of Mount Cook buttercups *(Ranunculus lyallii)*, a welcome contrast to the drab moraine of the Tasman Glacier stretched out below.

Follow the ridgecrest above, bypassing steeper sections wherever necessary on the eastern side. Slopes of scree and scrub are negotiated as the track heads steadily upwards, with ever-improving views to the high mountains at the head of the Tasman Glacier. As the broad sandstone ridge begins to level out, the privately owned Caroline Hut at 1790 metres soon comes into view just beyond a rocky basin. There is an emergency shelter built onto this hut, complete with a radio; toilets and water are also available for public use, but please respect the privacy of the people staying at the hut.

Allow two to three hours from the Ball Shelter to here.

The rocky knoll above Caroline Hut, known as Furggens Knob, can be ascended directly or bypassed to the south. Above this point, the ridge continues more or less directly towards the pass, with the ever-present backdrop of the Caroline Face of Aoraki/ Mt Cook for company. If you are lucky, some impressive avalanches may sweep down this huge face of steep ice.

The scramble along the upper reaches of the ridge leads, after about an hour, to an obvious descent onto the Ball Glacier below. This provides an easier route up to the pass, although there are a few narrow, transverse crevasses to negotiate; extra care should be taken after a fresh fall of snow, which could obscure these hazards.

Ball Pass, at 2121 metres, is gained after two to three hours from Caroline Hut by following the snow slope towards Turner Peak to the north, and then sidling up to the narrow crest of the ridge at its low point. Immediately below here, on the Tasman Valley side, are some narrow shelves of scree or snow that provide memorable camping spots in settled weather. However, be very aware that this pass is exposed to the full force of any westerly gales that may spring up during the night. Early in the season some parties build a snow cave up here; either way, respect the fragile nature of this alpine area and ensure that toilet waste in particular is buried well away from the pass itself.

Be sure not to miss the sunrise from this high mountain camp, as the East Face of Aoraki/Mt Cook catches

December sunrise on Aoraki/Mt Cook from Ball Pass camp

the first rays of the rising sun, followed soon after by the wall of mountains to the west and then the pass itself. For those with basic climbing skills, an early morning crampon ascent to Pt 2222 will give never-to-be-forgotten views all around New Zealand's premier alpine area.

The descent into the Hooker Valley from Ball Pass normally involves some travel on snow, which in the early morning will require the use of crampons and ice axes. This section is tricky in misty conditions, as the route is not straightforward from here.

The valley draining the pass leads to large bluffs and is not a recommended route, particularly in descent. The correct route, to the East Hooker, sidles on scree or snow slopes below Mt Rosa into the next basin to the south. It is important to cross the intervening ridge at the correct spot, otherwise further progress through a line of crags becomes problematic. A steady downward traverse leads below a rocky spur towards this intervening ridge. After you pass the toe of this spur, a short climb of about 100 metres leads back up to the ridge, which is crossed at around 1900 metres. There should be a large cairn marking this crossover point, although this sometimes disappears under snow during winter. It is some one-and-a-half hours from Ball Pass to this point.

From this vantage point, the lower section of the route is visible, leading into a narrow, rocky gully to the left (south) of a distinctive feature known locally as the Playing Fields. The terrain leading from the ridge down to this gully requires care, as there are bluffs to negotiate (these are considerably easier to tackle if you are coming up from the Hooker Valley).

Initially, traverse horizontally from the ridge to pick up a trail winding down through these bluffs to the scree slopes below, then head further down to the top of the obvious gully. The level Playing Fields are covered with fragile alpine plants, so tread carefully if you are planning to stop here and avoid camping on this spot, tempting though it may be.

The gully is long and reasonably steep, but leads directly down to the terraces above the Hooker Glacier and the track home. It is often snow-filled until December, and although the going is a lot easier on the knees in such conditions, you need to take care when the snow is frozen.

The 1000-metre descent from Ball Pass to these glacial terraces will take about three hours, while a further two to three hours along the cairned track will take you back to the carpark at the campground. A little way down the valley, the track crosses a small stream with a waterfall a short distance above. At the base of this fall is hidden a deep and narrow bathing pool, perfect for cooling sweaty bodies after the day's exertions.

Other delays to expect while wandering down this delightful track in springtime will be the stops to admire – and no doubt photograph – the rich displays of Mount Cook buttercups. These grow in great profusion along the banks of the crystal-clear streams that flow down through these shrub-covered terraces from the mountains above, providing a memorable contrast to the austere world of snow and ice experienced only a few hours before.

Dasler Pinnacles

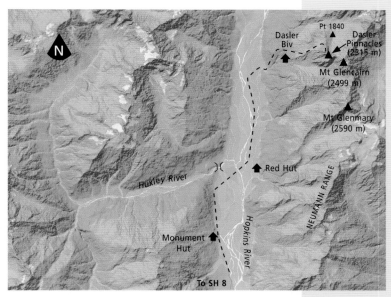

Duration: 2 days.

Grade: Moderate/rock scramble.

Time: 13–19 hours total, including ascent of Dasler Pinnacles. Monument Hut (6 bunks) to Dasler Bivvy (2 bunks): 4–5 hours. Dasler Bivvy to summit of Dasler Pinnacles: 3–5 hours. Dasler Bivvy to Monument Hut: 3–4 hours.

Maps: Ohau H38, Tasman H37.

Access: From SH 8 between Twizel and Omarama, turn onto Lake Ohau Lodge and ski field road. In the last few years this 50-km access road (sealed only as far as the lodge, 25 km) has been subject to periodic washouts for its last 8 km or so. Only sturdy 4WD vehicles can reach Monument Hut nowadays; otherwise, park near Huxley Lodge at the 'Road Closed' sign and either walk, or preferably mountain-bike, the final section of road to the hut and the start of the tramp. The walk along the road is a fairly dull 2 hours or more; biking is a lot faster and more fun, and bikes can be left outside Monument Hut. (Remember first to remove any soft temptations for marauding kea.)

Alternative Routes: There are a number of weekend tramps in this valley system – refer to the Ohau Conservation Area pamphlet.

Information: DoC Twizel, Ph: 03 435 0802.

WARNING! As this is an alpine area, some tracks can be subject to avalanches, particularly in winter and spring. Note also that the rivers are not always bridged and can be impassable during heavy rain.

The Hopkins Valley has a well-established network of tracks and huts, making it an ideal destination for a weekend trip away from the crowds at Aoraki/Mt Cook, just one range to the east. The valley floor offers relaxed trails through soft beech forests and across open river flats. The bushline and alpine areas above can be reached by a number of side tracks, providing rewarding panoramas over some fairly rugged country.

From Monument Hut (six bunks) a track leads through beech forest on the true right of the Hopkins Valley before dropping down onto grassy and stony flats. Alternatively, you can head directly onto the flats below the hut and head upvalley, crossing river braids where necessary. Either way, start to angle across this wide and expansive valley floor before you reach the junction with the Huxley River, which flows into the main valley from the west. The smooth, rocky, triangular outline of the Dasler Pinnacles soon comes into view across the valley, dominating the skyline to the northeast.

Mt Jackson, Elcho Pass and Mt Ward

In normal conditions the Hopkins River is sufficiently braided to present no problems, but flows will be higher during the spring melt and after heavy rain on the Main Divide. As with all river crossings, care and common sense should always be exercised.

The recently restored Red Hut (12 bunks) is clearly visible by the forest edge on the far side of the river. A good track can be picked up above this hut, following easy grassy flats – a pleasant change from the bouldery riverbed. It leads directly upvalley until a second side creek flows in from the east (true left), about three hours from Monument Hut.

The steep but relatively short climb up to the Dasler Biv (sometimes known as Cullers Biv) leaves the main valley at this point. After crossing the side stream (note that this is the last water before the biv), a large orange triangle at the bottom of the hillside shows the start of the track into the forest. The 500-metre climb up to the hut is initially very steep but well marked, negotiating a smooth slab (with fixed rope if you need it) after half an hour. Above here the angle relents somewhat, as the track ambles through mountain beech forest before crossing a small stream to the cosy two-bunk Dasler Biv, about one-and-a-half hours from the valley floor.

The biv is tucked into the bush edge and so doesn't have much of a view, but a 15-minute hike through subalpine scrub leads to sweeping panoramas down the multi-braided Hopkins Valley, across to the snowy peaks of the Main Divide and directly above to the jagged rock architecture of the Dasler Pinnacles. If a room with a view is your priority, or if by chance the bivvy is full, then good camping is possible up here.

The top of the Dasler Pinnacles can be reached via the shattered North Ridge, although this rock scramble requires a degree of skill plus a good head for heights. It follows the left-hand skyline ridge and is easier than it appears from below, but should only be tackled by confident parties in good weather.

From Dasler Biv, follow vague tracks up through scrub and tussock towards the obvious rocky knoll to the north of the main pinnacles (Pt 1840). Either climb over, or sidle around, this outlier to reach a shale plateau below the impressive West Face of the Daslers. There are a few roped climbing possibilities up these sweeping cliffs, but our route heads up scree slopes to the left, reaching a level spot where the North Ridge begins to steepen (allow two to three hours to this point).

The ridge is followed more or less directly to the top of the first pinnacle, invariably with a fair bit of loose rock and a high degree of exposure to the west. This section takes one to two hours, with a final, short scramble onto the main top via a narrow rock ridge. All around are impressive and dauntingly loose ridges and rock faces: Glencairn is a short distance along the ridge, while Glenisla lies across the deep valley to the north and Glenmary is to the south. The Main Divide peaks of Mts Ward and Jackson fill the skyline westwards.

The descent from this rocky summit is both easier and faster on the scree-covered ledges to the east of the ridge crest, thereby avoiding any tricky sections encountered during the ascent. A climb up the Daslers from the bivvy takes most parties between three and five hours, with the same for the descent, so be prepared for a long trip in total if you are planning to return to the road the same day. If a more relaxed weekend trip has been planned, then an excursion above the bivvy, perhaps as far as the rocky knoll previously mentioned, will give some great views as well as a close-up inspection of the Pinnacles above.

The return trip to the road can be varied a little by staying on the true left of the main Hopkins Valley until you are past Red Hut, and then cutting across the various river channels to Monument Hut.

Dasler Pinnacles

Brodrick Pass/Mt McKenzie

HUXLEY VALLEY

Duration: 2–3 days.

Grade: Moderate/easy mountain-eering.

Time: 18 hours total. Monument Hut (6 bunks) to Huxley Fork Huts (6 bunks, wood stove; 2 bunks): 3 hours. Huxley Fork Huts to Brodrick Hut (6 bunks): 2.5 hours. Brodrick Hut to Brodrick Pass: 2.5 hours. Brodrick Pass to Mt McKenzie: 2.5 hours. Mt McKenzie to Brodrick Hut: 2.5 hours. Brodrick Hut to Huxley Fork Huts: 2 hours. Huxley Fork Huts to Monument Hut: 3 hours.

Maps: Ohau H38, Tasman H37.

Access: See previous tramp (page 127).

Alternative Routes: The south branch of the Huxley Valley is also worth a visit.

Information: DoC Twizel, Ph: 03 435 0802.

WARNING! As this is an alpine area, some sections of the track can be subject to avalanches, particularly in winter and spring. There are a few, generally obvious, crevasses below Mt McKenzie. The ascent of Mt McKenzie from Brodrick Pass requires crampons and an ice axe, plus the skills to use them.

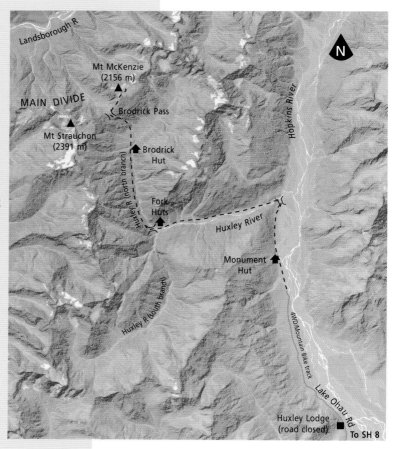

Despite the present washout about 8 kilometres short of the end of the access road, the Hopkins and Huxley valley systems are worthy of more than one weekend trip in this book. The area offers a wide variety of landscapes, from open river flats and gentle beech forest to rocky, snow-covered mountaintops. The Huxley Valley is a secluded side branch of the main Hopkins Valley (see previous tramp, page 127), with two well-maintained huts, a small bivvy and plenty of camping opportunities, and is quite feasible within a reasonably relaxed weekend.

A track leads into the forest by Monument Hut, and is followed for a short while before you drop down to the main river flats. A further half an hour leads to an obvious sign showing the way over a small forested spur to the Huxley River swingbridge.

130

Alternatively, the river can usually be waded without having to climb up to the bridge, thereby guaranteeing a wet-boot trip for the purists!

Once you are across the Huxley River, the track ambles easily along grassy flats on the north bank, having an almost 'European' feel about it (in other words, with no tree roots or mud), and offers extensive views both up and down the valley. A short ascent over a broad spur, followed by a gentle descent, leads to the adjacently situated new and old Huxley Fork Huts, reached after about two hours from the bridge. The new hut is a standard six-bunker with a wood stove, while the older and considerably more rustic one has only two bunks.

As the name of the huts implies, the Huxley Valley splits into a north and a south branch here, both of which are well worth exploring. The route to Brodrick Hut heads up the north branch, initially on a good forest trail to a swingbridge. It then sidles above the river on the true right, crossing a number of eroded and avalanche-scoured side creeks. The beech forest eventually thins out, to be replaced by a zone of sub-alpine scrub. The track descends to skirt the river again, before a final uphill climb to Brodrick Hut. This six-bunk hut is tucked away on the edge of the forest, having the advantage of shelter but the disadvantage of deep shade. However, the open fireplace, once cranked up, should alleviate any gloom on cold evenings, and views up to the wall of mountains at the head of the valley can be had just a stone's throw from the door.

Mt Trent and Upper Huxley from Brodrick Hut

Brodrick Pass is situated on the Main Divide and leads from the Hopkins/Huxley watershed into the less accessible Landsborough Wilderness Area, a mecca for trampers and hunters. The views from the pass itself are not that extensive, but an ascent of nearby Mt McKenzie will open up some unforgettable panoramas over the large peaks of the Landsborough.

Swingbridge on the Huxley River

It is a 600-metre climb from Brodrick Hut to the pass, and the track is well marked from the outset, crossing several loose gullies that cut through the sub-alpine scrub to the base of the pass. The path weaves between shoulder-high dracophyllum scrub to reach a zigzag trail that leads across tussock to the crest of the broad, sweeping pass itself. There are some fine camping possibilities next to the small tarns around the pass, where the well-watered alpine meadows are a haven for late-summer gentians. Views from here extend back down the verdant North Huxley Valley and across to Mt Strauchon, which overlooks the pass from the west.

Competent parties, familiar with the use of crampons and ice axes, can climb the relatively straightforward peak of Mt McKenzie, situated just to the north. Start by skirting below a rocky ridge on gentle snow slopes before climbing directly up a small glacier with a few obvious crevasses. This leads to the main ridge, with the 2156-metre-high summit at the western end (allow about two hours or so from the pass). The views from Mt McKenzie across the mighty Landsborough Valley to the Solution Range and Mts Hooker, Dechen and Strachan are a just reward for the effort, while to the northeast along the Main Divide the Aoraki/Mt Cook Range stands proud on the horizon.

An easier descent can be made by heading over a small snow dome to the east and then straight down the broad, crevasse-free South Ridge (this could, of course, be used for the ascent). The route down to the valley floor and beyond is the same as for the way up, although invariably a lot faster. Allow two-and-a-half hours from the summit to Brodrick Hut and a further two hours to the Huxley Forks.

Brewster Hut/Mt Armstrong

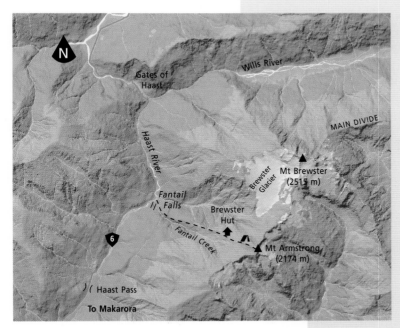

Duration: 2 days.

Grade: Moderate.

Time: 9–12 hours total. Carpark to Brewster Hut (4–6 bunks): 3–4 hours. Brewster Hut to Mt Armstrong: 2–3 hours. Mt Armstrong to carpark: 4–5 hours.

Maps: Haast Pass G38, Mount Aspiring Parkmap 273/02.

Access: From Fantail Falls carpark on the Haast Highway (SH 6).

Information: DoC Makarora, Ph 03 443 8365 (closed in winter); DoC Wanaka, Ph 03 443 7660.

Mount Aspiring National Park has a rich variety of tramping possibilities, although many of them take several days to complete. This rewarding two-day trip leads directly to the alpine zone above the Haast Pass road, and to a small, cosy hut not far above the bushline. Alternatively, spectacular campsites are available higher up the mountainside, offering extensive views across the deep Haast Valley below to Mt Aspiring and nearby Mt Brewster, with its dazzling white-ice glacier. Once a base has been established, this is the perfect spot for some leisurely exploration.

From the carpark, take the track down to Fantail Falls and cross the Haast River about 100 metres downstream. If river levels are low, it is worth wading barefoot since the rest of the trip is a dry-boot rarity.

The track into shady beech forest is signposted at the start and continues to be well marked as it climbs steeply away from the valley floor to emerge, after about two hours, at the bushline. A further hour or so is spent weaving up the snowgrass face, with ever-improving vistas to the south, before you reach the Brewster Hut (sleeps four to six, but there are no cooking facilities). This is situated at a flat spot on the ridge next to some small tarns, and as it is of only very modest size it can soon become crowded.

In settled weather consider bringing a tent instead, as this will provide the flexibility this area deserves. Continue above the hut towards the rocky 'tramper's peak' of Mt

Armstrong (2174 metres), where occasional tarns provide the necessary water for an overnight camp. There are some great little spots among these alpine meadows, where the uninterrupted views south to Mt Aspiring and other lofty neighbours more than compensate for the extra climb and heavier pack. Settle down for an evening among the high mountains and enjoy a West Coast sunset from this vantage point.

The morning would be well spent scrambling up among the schist outcrops of Mt Armstrong. In late summer the small tarns and rocky pools below this peak are thick with creamy clusters of alpine gentians, among other flowers. The view from the summit extends far and wide, with the distinctive massifs of Aoraki/Mt Cook and Mt Sefton to the north, and Mts Aspiring and Earnslaw to the south, along with the peaks of the Wilkin Valley. An ascent of Mt Brewster itself requires mountaineering skills and is normally attempted from the glacier or the ridge above it.

Return by the same route, passing the hut before making the short, sharp descent through the beech forest down to the river and the Haast Highway. Your screaming thighs and aching knees can be cooled off under the refreshing Fantail Falls, so long as the flow is moderate. A perfect plunge pool away from the snapping cameras below is located halfway up the falls and is accessed by scrambling up slabs on the true right.

Evening view of Mt Brewster, Mount Aspiring National Park

West Matukituki Valley

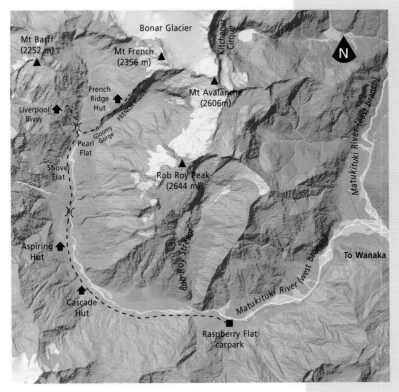

Duration: 2 days.

Grade: Moderate.

Time: 15–16 hours total. Raspberry Flat to Aspiring Hut (30 bunks): 2.5 hours. Aspiring Hut to French Ridge Hut (17 bunks): 4–5 hours. French Ridge Hut to Aspiring Hut via Liverpool Bivvy (6 bunks): 6 hours.

Maps: Aspiring E39, Mount Aspiring Parkmap 273/02.

Access: Drive 60 km from Wanaka along the western shore of Lake Wanaka to the carpark at Raspberry Flat. For transport to the start of the track, contact Wanaka Information Centre for details, Ph 03 443 1233.

Alternative Routes: A short distance from the Raspberry Flat carpark, a side track leads down to a swingbridge across the river and up the Rob Roy Valley. This is a justifiably popular day trip from Wanaka and is worth incorporating into any tramping plans in the area.

Information: DoC Wanaka, Ph 03 443 7660.

WARNING! As this is an alpine area, some tracks can be subject to avalanches, particularly in winter and spring.

The well-established tracks along the Matukituki Valley enable trampers to get into the heart of the Mount Aspiring National Park, while two large and one not-so-large huts provide a good standard of accommodation in this popular region. On this route, easy travel on the flats contrasts with some steep mountainside tracks to reach a couple of perfectly situated huts perched high above the valley floor, both with excellent panoramic views from their front doors.

The carpark at Raspberry Flat gets quite busy in the summer months, and has new toilets, a shelter and an information panel. The public road ends here, and although a 4WD track continues upvalley, this provides access for farm vehicles only. The walk up to Aspiring Hut (two to two-and-a-half hours) frequently follows these tracks, cutting a few corners where possible. It is a very gentle walk alongside the river, or across the terraces above, but the views all around the majestic Matukituki

French Ridge Hut and Mt Avalanche

Valley make it a memorable introduction to the region. This section could also easily be mountain-biked in about an hour, as the national park boundary is not reached until Aspiring Hut.

From Raspberry Flat, the track continues up the wide, gentle valley for an hour or so, before being forced to climb over a forested bluff with the impressive Brides Veil Falls high on the hillside above. About half an hour further on, a small hut by the bush edge is passed. This is Cascade Hut, and is owned by the Otago section of the New Zealand Alpine Club (NZAC); unlike the club's other huts further up the valley, this one is kept locked, and is available by prior booking only.

Another half-hour across the grassy flats takes you to the far more substantial Aspiring Hut, which sleeps up to 30 trampers and climbers. This hut is a solidly constructed, large stone building dating back to the late 1950s, and although owned by the NZAC it is administered by DoC. In the summer months there is a warden in residence to collect hut fees ($20 per night for non-members at the time of writing) and gas cookers are provided. There is also solar lighting, plus flush toilets in the newly built ablutions block. All this, plus views up to the southern aspects of Mt Aspiring, which pokes its head above the intervening forested ridges, makes it an ideal base even if you are not planning to stay further up the valley. A day shelter and campsites are also provided just a couple of minutes beyond the hut. Note, however, that Aspiring Hut does get busy in summer, as it is also the starting point for the trip over Cascade Saddle and into the Rees/Dart valley systems.

Continuing up the Matukituki Valley, the track crosses Cascade Creek and then Rough Creek on solid bridges before breaking out of the beech forest onto Shovel Flat after about an hour. At the northern end of this wide grassy clearing, the track re-enters bush for a short distance before a second clearing, Pearl Flat, is reached after a further half-hour. There is a choice of routes from this point; both of those described here involve a fairly stiff climb of between 500 and 900 metres from the valley floor.

The route up to French Ridge Hut (1480 metres) starts with a wade across the usually shallow Matukituki River to its true left bank, although if it is running high a swingbridge located upstream can be utilised (this adds half an hour to the trip). A well-marked track enters the forest at the bottom of the steep hillside confronting you, and is a fairly strenuous affair, involving pulling yourself up with the help of handy tree roots as height is rapidly gained towards the bushline. This takes between one and one-and-a-half hours, at which point the rather brutal angle so far encountered eases off somewhat as the track meanders through subalpine scrub. The views across the valley to the diminutive Liverpool Bivvy and Mt Barff, or up into the ravine on the right (known as Gloomy Gorge), with Mt Avalanche at its head, are a welcome distraction from the climb through dracophyllum and totara bushes.

After about an hour along this narrowing and obvious ridgeline, which is very exposed to the elements in bad weather, the large, red, French Ridge Hut comes into view. This is situated on a small level section of the ridge and is a recent replacement for the much older huts and bivvies that have occupied this site since 1940. This hut is

Shovel Flat, Mount Aspiring National Park

also owned by NZAC and operated by DoC, and once again a warden is often around over summer to make sure the place runs smoothly. As it lies on the route to the Bonar Glacier and Mt Aspiring, the hut does see a fair amount of through traffic during the season, as weary climbers return from the heights above. It sleeps 17 and offers outstanding views from its balcony (fees at the time of writing are $15 per night for non-members).

The ridge above the hut can safely be followed to the snowline for evening views across the deep valley and mountains beyond (allow an hour). The panoramas just get better, with Mts Athene, Ionia and Eros appearing above the remote Arawhata Valley to the west, while the tumbling icefall of the Bonar Glacier spills over the Breakaway directly to the north. Travel beyond the permanent snowline and up the Quarterdeck to the Bonar Glacier should only be attempted by suitably equipped and experienced parties; there are some sizeable crevasses cutting across this narrow lead of ice.

The return to the valley floor will be a lot quicker for those trampers used to knee-wrecking descents, otherwise allow one-and-a-half hours to reach the river far below.

The trip up to Liverpool Bivvy, on the opposite side of the valley, is a mere 550-metre climb from the valley floor, and a fine way to get a feel for both sides of the Matukituki Valley. If you are only planning to visit this cosy little hut for lunch (although it is worth a night here, given time), then lighten your load by hiding your pack in the forest away from the ever-active keas. Cross a bridge over Liverpool Stream, a short distance beyond which a track is signposted into the forest. It takes between one-and-a-half and two hours up this steep and obvious route, with more tree-root pull-ups, to reach the six-bunk biv. Avoid any urges to cut across the deep gully directly to the hut when it comes into view, as this leads into some very rough country. Instead, follow the well-trodden path over a rocky knob before descending to the picturesquely situated biv and neighbouring small tarn. Note that sections of the track above the bushline are steep and exposed, so great care should be taken in wet or icy conditions.

Liverpool Bivvy is perched on the edge of a grassy shelf overlooking the valley far below. Directly opposite, across the valley, rises the graceful icy pyramid of Mt Aspiring, at 3030 metres the highest peak outside of the Aoraki/Mount Cook and Westland/Tai Poutini national parks, and one of the most popular 3000-metre summits in the country. There is limited exploring to be had from the bivvy – a trip up to Arawhata Saddle is quite a serious and tricky proposition, as are the lower schist slabs of Mt Barff directly above. A better option would be to relax and soak up the views before returning down to the river and back out to Aspiring Hut.

Wye Creek

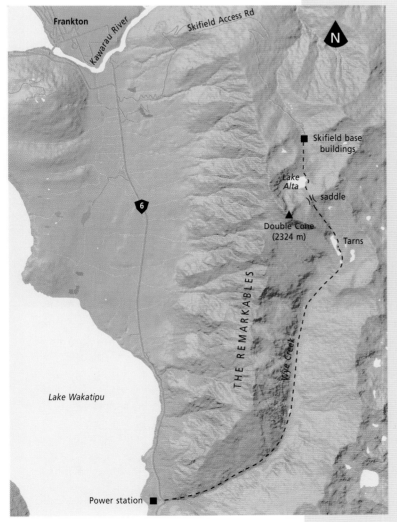

Duration: 1 day.

Grade: Moderate.

Time: 8–10 hours.

Maps: Arrowtown F41, Kingston F42.

Access: Remarkables skifield road, off SH 6 between Frankton and Kingston.

Alternative Routes: Although this trip can be done in one day, the tarns towards the head of Wye Valley would make excellent campsites, allowing plenty of time to explore the crags and ridges overhead.

Information: DoC Queenstown, Ph 03 442 7932.

WARNING! Snow patches can linger around Lake Alta and the saddle well into summer – take care when these are frozen.

The accessible yet oddly remote Wye Creek Valley lies tucked away to the east of Lake Wakatipu, within easy reach of Queenstown for a longish day trip. A feeling of alpine isolation pervades the upper reaches of the valley, and yet only the sawtooth ridge of the Remarkables separates it from the glitz and glamour of the resort across the lake. By starting at the skifield carpark (1600 metres) and finishing by the shores of Lake Wakatipu (360 metres), the only major climb of the day is the 360 metres up to the Wye Saddle. However, as there is a 40-minute drive between the start and finish of this

Double Cone and tarns, Upper Wye Valley

hike, some prior transport arrangements are called for. This trip is only suitable for tramping parties in the snow-free months of summer.

The skifield road is open all year round, and allows for easy access to the alpine environment of the Remarkables. The drive up to the carpark takes about 20 minutes from the main turn-off on SH 6.

The track climbs steadily from the carpark along the true right of the Alta chairlift to reach Lake Alta in an easy hour. The lake is a classic alpine jewel, nestled in a glacial cirque and surrounded by steep schistose crags, popular with rock climbers in the summer months. Skirt around the lake to the south and ascend a vague zigzag track up boulder-covered scree slopes to the obvious saddle. From here, the highest point of the day, drop down into the wide, tarn-studded basin of the Upper Wye Creek, a magnificent alpine area overlooked by the impressive pyramid of Double Cone, standing sentinel at the head of the valley.

Angle down leftwards, passing a number of tarns, until you find yourself above a 100-metre-high waterslide, which drains the large tarn above. The route, occasionally cairned, drops steeply down the true left of this waterfall to the valley floor. It is also possible to sidle quite high along exposed ledges from the top of the waterfall, initially with some steep bluffs directly below. Once these give out, the valley floor can be reached by descending boulder and tussock slopes.

The route now follows the true left bank of Wye Creek, picking up vague trails and sporadic cairns through waist-high tussock punctuated with impressive clumps of spaniards and a few marshy sections. After about two hours the valley narrows into a rocky gorge, where the creek tumbles down a series of waterfalls. The track contours above this gorge until Lake Wakatipu comes into view, framed by the steep valley sides.

The track now leads down to Wye Creek, crossing to a newly cut trail on the far bank via a small, scrubby island splitting the river. Cairns mark the track into beech forest, where a well-signed trail leads down to the Wye Creek hydro intake before zig-zagging past a number of schistose crags to reach the main highway along the eastern shore of Lake Wakatipu.

Large tarn in the Upper Wye Valley

Ben Lomond/Arthurs Point

Duration: 1 day.

Grade: Easy.

Time: 7 hours total. One Mile Creek carpark to Ben Lomond: 3 hours. Ben Lomond to Arthurs Point township: 4 hours.

Map: Queenstown E41.

Access: Lomond Crescent, Queenstown.

Information: DoC Queenstown, Ph 03 442 7932.

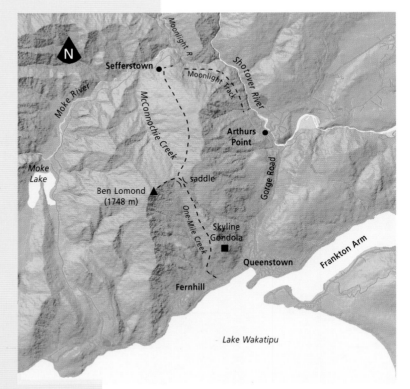

An ascent of Ben Lomond is a very popular day trip from Queenstown, offering extensive views over the Wakatipu Basin and northwards to Mts Aspiring and Earnslaw. For some reason, however, the round trip to Arthurs Point is less frequented, but it is well worth the extra effort to avoid backtracking. There are at least half a dozen Ben Lomonds in New Zealand; this one is nearly 800 metres higher than its Scottish Highland namesake.

Note that this walk crosses private land, so please respect this and leave gates as you find them. As there is no water along the walk, remember to take plenty with you.

The steep climb up from the town can be avoided by taking the Skyline Gondola to an alternative start for the Ben Lomond track. However, the purist approach is up One Mile Creek, which starts near the end of Lomond Crescent, a short hike from the town centre.

Small pockets of native bush soon give way to gloomy stands of Douglas fir, which at least provide shade on a hot day. After an hour in the forest you reach the bushline, from where the track strikes out across open tussockland.

The ascent is gradual to Ben Lomond Saddle, but the final 45 minutes to the

1748-metre-high summit are steep and rocky. The view from the top, over Queenstown, the lake and endless ranges stretching in all directions is quite spectacular, and certainly puts the town in a different perspective. There is a plane-table on the summit to help identify all those unknown mountains spanning the horizon.

Descend back to the saddle, from where a poled route sidles across tussock slopes way above McConnochie Creek. This eventually leads down to the old goldmining settlement of Sefferstown; in fact, this entire area is steeped in history dating back to the gold-rush period of the 1860s. However, if you stay high above the junction of the Moke and Moonlight rivers, a farm track is gained, which contours above the true right side of the Shotover River. This leads down to Arthurs Point township and a cooling jug of ale at the local pub.

Near the top of Ben Lomond, with Moke Lake below

Takitimu Range

Duration: 2 days.

Grade: Moderate.

Time: 8.5 hours total. Pleasant Creek to Aparima Hut (8 bunks, potbelly stove): 2 hours. Aparima Hut to Aparima Forks Hut (2 bunks): 2.5 hours. Aparima Forks Hut to Dunrobin Valley Road: 4 hours.

Map: Takitimu D44.

Access: From SH 94 at Mossburn, take Otautau Road for 10 km before turning into Dunrobin Road. This road is 25 km long, its last 10 km unsealed. The track starts by the small wooden bridge over Pleasant Creek, where you can park your car.

Alternative Routes: An alternative return route in fine weather heads from the Aparima Forks Hut over Clare Peak and down Waterloo Burn to Aparima Hut (allow 10–11 hours).

Information: DoC Invercargill, Ph 03 214 4589; DoC Te Anau, Ph 03 249 7924.

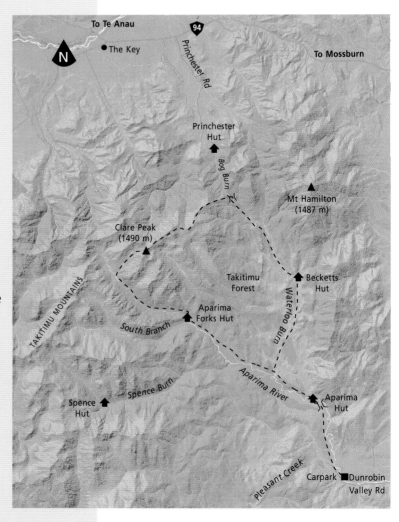

The Takitimu Mountains are the rugged line of 1600-metre-plus hills passed by speeding tourists on their way from Queenstown to Milford. Situated southwest of Mossburn, and well away from the main Fiordland mountains, they tend to get far better weather than the ranges further west. Despite this distinct advantage in a region of such weather extremes, they are surprisingly neglected, except by locally based trampers and hunters, who have discovered the uncrowded pleasures of these quiet backwaters. The area offers a good network of tracks and simple huts down in the valleys, as well as some travel along the extensive ridgetops during the snow-free months of summer.

The start of the track is signposted from Pleasant Creek and generally follows the true right bank of the Aparima River. During the initial 15–20 minutes you pass through scrubby stands of matagouri and along flood-damaged sections of riverbank littered with debris – evidence that, even away from the Main Divide, rainfall in this area can sometimes be extreme. This rough section can be avoided by following the boundary fence with Pleasant Valley Farm as far as a woolshed, and then heading down to the riverbank.

The track soon improves, with markers generally leading along the riverbank through patches of manuka scrub, which are somewhat overgrown, and into stands of beech forest. The open clearings are usually quite damp underfoot and support a rich variety of wetland species, in particular vivid green clumps of bog pine (*Halocarpus bidwillii*). The extensive fields of waving red tussock offer a particularly fine display of colour, especially when contrasted with the snowy tops in springtime.

There is evidence of 4WD tracks coming in from the river terraces above, which although extremely rough and boggy would seem to be accessible for off-road enthusiasts. After you meet up with one of these tracks the Aparima Hut soon comes into view, perched on a terrace across the river. The hut (with eight bunks and a potbelly stove) is reached via a swingbridge just downstream, then along the tussocky terrace by the fenceline.

Tussock below the Takitimu Range

Aparima Hut, Takitimu Range

Continuing up the main valley, the track climbs away from the hut to overlook an extensive area of marshy flats, across which meanders the Waterloo Burn. There is a track up this valley, which passes Becketts Hut (four bunks) and crosses over a low saddle to reach the northern roadend at Princhester Hut (six bunks) after about six hours.

An alternative, as described here, carries on along the old river terrace, past a trig point at 564 metres, before heading down to an obvious sharp bend in the river, marked with erosion scars and slips. Entering a stand of mature beech trees, the track continues within earshot of the river below. The going in some of the clearings is very boggy, with thick carpets of sphagnum moss squelching underfoot. It is better to enjoy this sensation rather than attempt to avoid the quagmires – a virtual impossibility in these parts. The largest of the peat bogs is located at the junction with the Spence Burn, at which point another track heads off to the Spence Hut. Skirt around the toe of this clearing, keeping close to the margin, before re-entering the forest.

The mossy forest trail continues to a point where the Aparima River can easily be crossed to the true right bank. The Aparima Forks Hut has only two bunks, but would make a suitable night's stop for a small party.

From the Aparima Forks Hut there is easy travel to the heads of both branches of the Aparima River, both of which are suitable for exploration if you plan to return back down the valley. The return via the route you followed in takes about four hours.

A good alternative return route in fine weather leads from the bushline, which is reached about one-and-a-half hours from the hut. This traverses Clare Peak (1490 metres) and heads down to Waterloo Burn, about three to four hours beyond the Aparima Valley bushline. From the saddle, drop down to the burn itself; following it mainly along its left bank, you pass Becketts Hut (four bunks), hidden in the forest, after two hours. The going is easy but quite boggy across the tussock-covered valley floor to the Aparima Hut, gained after a further one-and-a-half hours.

This alternative return makes an excellent round trip over the rocky tops and marshy valleys of the Takitimus if the weather is good. It does, however, make for a long day – allow 10 to 11 hours to reach Dunrobin Valley Road from Aparima Forks Hut.

The Takitimus from the slopes of Mt Titiroa

Moraine Creek/Adelaide Basin

FIORDLAND NATIONAL PARK

Duration: 2–3 days.

Grade: Hard (route-finding skills required).

Time: 15–18 hours total. Lower Hollyford Road to Phil's Bivvy (sleeps 10): 8–10 hours. Phil's Bivvy to Lower Hollyford Road: 7–8 hours.

Map: Milford D40.

Access: Lower Hollyford Road, off the Milford Highway.

Alternative Routes: For those with a good head for heights and basic mountaineering skills, it is possible to make a round trip from the Lower Hollyford Road to Gertrude Valley via Lake Adelaide, Barrier Knob and Gertrude Saddle. A trip among these jagged ranges rewards the transalpine tramper with unsurpassable views over a particularly rugged part of Fiordland.

Information: DoC Te Anau, Ph 03 249 7924.

Warning! Avalanches potentially threaten many parts of this trip in winter and spring, especially where the route skirts close under steep cliffs.

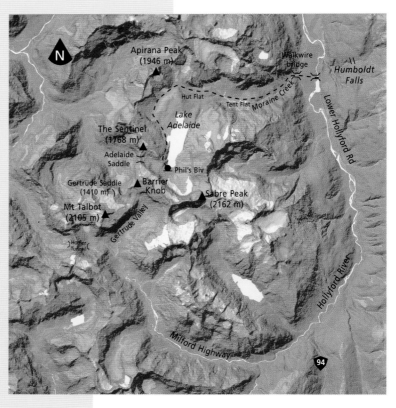

The Adelaide Basin is one of the few places in the Darran Mountains that can easily be reached by non-mountaineers. It is also one of the most spectacular glacial cirques, being hemmed in on three sides by towering Fiordland cliffs and hanging glaciers. Access for trampers is via Moraine Creek, which drains the basin, as other approaches require varying degrees of mountaineering skill. The presence of a palatial bivvy rock is also a bonus in a part of the country where rainfall is legendary.

The Moraine Creek track starts by the Lower Hollyford Road, just upvalley from the Humboldt Falls carpark. Cross the main Hollyford River over a substantial swingbridge and follow the track to a smaller three-wire bridge over Moraine Creek.

Charlie Gifford, who accompanied Fiordland explorer William Graves on his 1908/09 summer expedition, suggested the correct spelling of this creek ought to be 'More Rain Creek'. They did, after all, experience 13 wet days in the first fortnight of their journey into this area during midsummer. Even in today's Gore-Tex era it would be prudent to postpone a trip into these parts until fair weather is forecast.

Climb steeply through dense Fiordland forest on a reasonable track, which offers the usual combination of slippery tree roots, mossy boulders and mud! After three hours of thick forest travel, a sizeable – and swimmable – tarn is reached near the bushline. Shortly afterwards, the track crosses the open tussock basin of Tent Flat, following a poled route across these marshy clearings (there are some good campsites on the forest edge).

As you re-enter the forest, the beech trees soon begin to give way to a mix of ribbonwood, mountain holly and prickly shield fern. An impressive waterfall issuing from the Korako Glacier basin can now be seen to the north.

Aim for a low saddle between the forested moraine ridge (which forms the dam for Lake Adelaide, still hidden above) and the steep cliffs on the true left by angling away from the valley floor. The track is at times indistinct, but a small streambed provides good access to the tussock pastures above, with occasional cairns to show the way.

Another open area, Hut Flat, is reached after about five hours from the road. This is the site of the old Moraine Creek Hut, which was destroyed by an avalanche many

Mt Adelaide and Sabre Peak, Fiordland National Park

years ago. A small bivvy rock is located on the lower side of this flat, near the edge of the forest and main stream.

Keep tucked in under the steep cliffs of Revelation Peak, following a small, usually dry, creekbed to the saddle in the moraine dam, from where a short descent leads to muddy flats and a small tarn. Avoid the masses of scrub-covered boulders between here and Lake Adelaide by skirting hard under the cliffs on the true left, passing above a number of small tarns where there is some camping available.

The view up the valley from here is quite stunning, with the large, solid pyramid of Sabre Peak drawing the eye ever upwards. An ascent of this peak is something of a Holy Grail for mountaineers. Flanking the monolith are the impressive north faces of Mts Marian and Adelaide, which provide a fairly impassable wall for mere mortals!

The route to Phil's Bivvy passes through a section of scrubby boulder field before a cairn marks the start of an 80-metre climb to the obvious terrace above the lake. This is followed, with a few slabby interruptions, to the outlet of the so-called Lake South America, the smaller lake below Adelaide Saddle and unnamed on the map.

Phil's Bivvy lies amongst the most obvious and largest cluster of four enormous boulders high on the slope below Barrier Knob and is reached by contouring above the ribbonwood and tussock scrub. This palatial bivouac site has a choice of two rooms and levelled sleeping platforms with enough room for 10 or more. It was named by Darrans climbers in memory of Phil Herron, a young activist in these parts in the 1970s whose mountaineering career was sadly cut short by a Patagonian crevasse in 1975. Lower down towards the lake is another bivvy rock, known as Gill's Bivvy, which is situated about 200 metres from the outlet of Lake South America.

On the lower sections of Moraine Creek, looking downvalley to the Hollyford River

Outside Phil's Bivvy with Lake Adelaide beyond

The Adelaide Basin, a most impressive alpine cirque, is ideally worth a day's exploration, using the bivvy rock as a base. A walk up to the meadows below the monolithic North Buttress of Sabre, a trip towards Adelaide Saddle or even a scramble up the Sentinel for those with sufficient experience would be a day well spent. Routes up Gifford Crack to Adelaide Saddle and over Barrier Knob to the Gertrude Valley are true mountaineering routes, and would make a splendid round trip for those with sufficient experience and a good head for heights

Alternatively, the way out of the Adelaide Basin follows the route of ascent – remember to keep well left above the lake, thereby avoiding the elephantine boulder fields below. The track down to Hut Flat and into the forest must be correctly located to avoid any mishaps. As with any less well-marked track in the mountains, you should have made mental notes of recognisable landmarks on the approach walk.

Gertrude Saddle/Barrier Knob

FIORDLAND NATIONAL PARK

Duration: 1 day.

Grade: Moderate/scramble.

Time: 8–10 hours total. Milford Highway to Gertrude Saddle: 3–4 hours. Gertrude Saddle to Barrier Knob: 1 hour.

Map: Milford D40.

Access: Gertrude Valley turn-off from Milford Highway, 1 km east of Homer Tunnel.

Information: DoC Te Anau, Ph 03 249 7924.

WARNING! This route is very exposed to avalanches in winter and spring, as huge accumulations of snow can build up on the steep shelves above the valley. Be aware of the potential avalanche risk at all times.

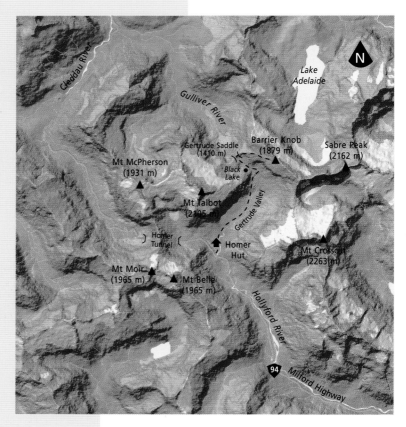

The Darran Mountains, passed en route to Milford Sound, offer only limited opportunities for the average tramper to penetrate their rocky precipices. The Gertrude Valley is an exception to this, providing a straightforward, although strenuous, day trip into the heart of the Fiordland mountains. The track leads you with relative ease into a rugged landscape of sheer rock faces, hanging snowfields and icy mountain lakes. When combined with a scramble up Barrier Knob, the route rewards the tramper with some excellent mountain panoramas into the mighty Adelaide Basin and down to Milford Sound.

The track up the Gertrude Valley starts about a kilometre east of the Homer Tunnel mouth at a large carpark near the Homer Hut. This New Zealand Alpine Club hut provides the only accommodation in the area, and can sleep up to 45 people. It is open to non-members, and has a wood stove and, usually, gas cookers. A warden is often resident during the summer months and, at the time of writing, there are plans for a major upgrade of this classic, 37-year-old mountaineers' hut.

Starting from the carpark, follow cairns across and along dry watercourses, through some shady patches of beech forest to the open valley above. The track continues along the valley floor through dense alpine herbfields, a visual delight in the summer months, before climbing steeply up towards Black Lake. A well-trodden trail leads alongside a tumbling stream before crossing below a waterfall to the true left bank. Continue uphill to reach a section of smooth rock slabs (slippery when wet or icy), across which cairns mark the way. There are some fixed cables for the final section of rock scrambling, which leads abruptly to a perfectly situated glacial lake nestled in an ice-scoured bowl of Fiordland gabbro.

Although never warm, Black Lake on a hot summer's day is a swimming hole never to be forgotten. Above the lake, after a further half-hour of smooth slabs (plus in situ cables at the start) and some bouldery scrambling, you reach the 1410-metre-high Gertrude Saddle. Look out for the elusive but frequently heard rock wrens that live among the boulder fields at these altitudes.

The view from the saddle northwards down Gulliver Valley is a classic example of the glaciation that has moulded so much of the dramatic scenery in Fiordland. The U-shaped valley below would have been filled with ice as recently as 8000 years ago, and in places the vegetation has yet to fully colonise the recently exposed bedrock.

Most people are happy to stop at this point and soak up the view, but there are

Towards Milford Sound, from Barrier Knob

options to explore further afield on either side of the saddle. A few hundred metres to the south are some alpine tarns, which are shallower than Black Lake and therefore slightly warmer propositions for a cooling dip.

Barrier Knob is 470 metres above the saddle, and can be climbed in good weather by competent rock scramblers. Follow the vague trail leading up to the northeast, avoiding any lingering snow patches and sticking to the beautiful, rough gabbro to reach the blocky summit in an hour or two.

From here, the views over the Darrans are magnificent, with Mt Tutuko, the highest peak in Fiordland, dominating the horizon along with its equally ice-draped companion, Mt Madeline. Directly below the summit of Barrier Knob is the large basin occupied by Lake Adelaide, itself ringed with an array of impressive peaks. The upper section of the route into this basin via Moraine Creek can be observed from this vantage point (see previous tramp, page 148).

Return to the Milford Highway by the same route, keeping an eye open for cairns that mark the best route off Barrier Knob and across the smooth rock slabs below Gertrude Saddle.

On Gertrude Saddle looking towards Milford Sound

Mt Titiroa

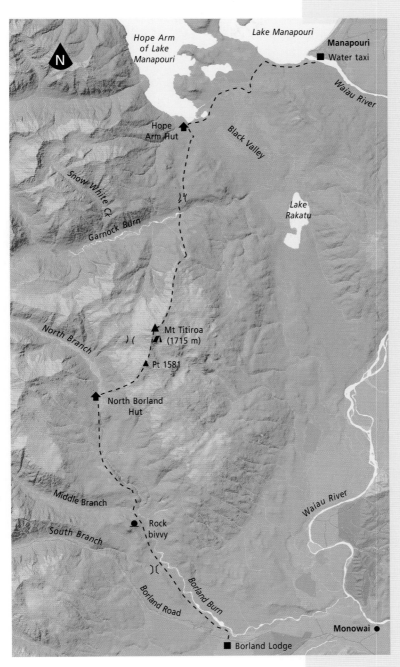

Hope Arm
of Lake
Manapouri

Lake Manapouri

Manapouri
■ Water taxi

N

Waiau River

Hope
Arm Hut

Black Valley

Snow White Ck

Garnock Burn

Lake
Rakatu

North Branch

▲ Mt Titiroa
(1715 m)

▲ Pt 1581

▲ North Borland
Hut

Middle Branch

South Branch

● Rock
bivvy

Borland Road

Borland Burn

Waiau River

Monowai ●

■ Borland Lodge

Duration: 2–3 days.

Grade: Hard (route-finding skills required).

Time: 17–19 hours total. Pearl Harbour to Hope Arm Hut (12 bunks, wood fire): 2–3 hours. Hope Arm Hut to Garnock Burn: 2 hours. Garnock Burn to Mt Titiroa: 5 hours. Mt Titiroa to North Borland Hut (2 bunks): 3–4 hours. North Borland Hut to Borland Lodge: 5 hours.

Maps: Manapouri C43, Hunter Mountains C44.

Access: Water taxi or rowboat from Manapouri (Pearl Harbour) across the Waiau River. Water taxi or boat hire can be arranged from the Manapouri Stores, Ph 03 249 6619.

Alternative Routes: If the weather is bad on the tops, Mt Titiroa itself can be bypassed via a saddle crossing over from Garnock Burn to the north branch of the Borland Valley.

Information: DoC Te Anau, Ph 03 249 7924. Borland Lodge, Ph 03 225 5464

As you approach Te Anau from the north, Mt Titiroa is the prominent peak rising above Lake Manapouri, appearing always to have a light dusting of fresh snow on its isolated summit. This is a result of geology rather than climate, as the summit ridge is scattered with remarkable, light-coloured granite formations and associated extensive scree slopes. The peak can be climbed from Manapouri in two days, and offers a superb viewpoint over the Fiordland mountains and lakes. As the summit of Mt Titiroa is too far to be reached comfortably from the Hope Arm Hut in a day, take a tent so that you can camp en route.

A water-taxi ride directly to the hut at Hope Arm will save two to three hours' walk, although the track through majestic stands of silver beech and twisted rimu from Pearl Harbour is a pleasant introduction to the lush and relatively bird-rich forests of Fiordland. The boggier sections along the well-graded track are crossed with board-walk, before you arrive at Hope Arm and the hut, at the far end of the beach.

The track continues directly behind the hut, leaving the lowland forest and climbing steadily to a more twisted and stunted 'goblin forest', with sections of upland swamp. A flat saddle is crossed before the track drops steeply to Garnock Burn.

The best way onto the North Ridge of Mt Titiroa is to climb the forested hillside directly across the Garnock Burn from where the Hope Arm track exits the bush. This is steep, with no obvious track and a few bluffs that need to be bypassed, although less than an hour of struggle will lead you to the more open ridgetop. From this point, a well-defined ground trail leads southwards, up through a delightful moss-carpeted forest of dwarf beech and bog pine to the abrupt bushline, some two hours from the valley floor.

The main rock-strewn North Ridge of Mt Titiroa is accessed via a gentle, sandy saddle, with a reliable water source and adequate camping spots. This would make a good base for climbing the mountain if you plan to return to Manapouri rather than traversing the peak to the Borland Valley. From this point onwards, the route is very exposed to the elements and has longish sections without regular water, although this precious commodity can often be found filling eroded rockpools on the giant boulders that lie scattered along the ridgetop.

The climb between, over, or around this array of weirdly shaped granite boulders is a photographer's paradise, framed by the backdrop of Lake Manapouri, now far below. Centuries of exposure to wind, rain and cycles of freeze-thaw have created a unique landscape of highly weathered quartz-rich granite tors. This terrain is some-what akin to that of the Dry Valleys in Antarctica, where similar climatic conditions and associated weathering processes have produced a comparable landscape of bizarre rock sculptures.

There are a few small tarns to the east, in sheltered basins below the main ridge, which would provide good campsites within easy striking distance of the summit early the following day. Alternatively, push on to the top for spectacular evening panoramas over some of the wilder parts of Fiordland, although this makes for a long, 10-hour day from Manapouri. Water and a campsite can be found directly below the summit, on a narrow, sandy shelf with great views across to the Takitimus and northwards to Mts Tutuko and Earnslaw.

From the 1715-metre-high summit of Mt Titiroa, the ridge continues southwards to provide a fine scramble along its rocky crest, although some of the steeper sections are more safely bypassed on its eastern side. On a clear day the views extend over the Hunter Mountains, with Stewart Island lying hazily on the southern horizon.

Sooner or later these panoramas have to be left behind, as it is necessary to drop down to North Borland Hut in the valley far below. From Pt 1581 a broad ridge heads down in a southwesterly direction to a cluster of tarns near the bushline. There is no obvious track through the forest below, although by following a spur on the true left of the creek that drains these tarns, a route can be found to the valley floor. The bush is initially quite dense, its thickets of beech, totara and bog pine negotiable with the help of gravity, but soon more open forest is reached, with a delightfully springy carpet of moss to ease sore knees. North Borland Hut is a small, two-person corrugated-iron structure sited on a terrace just above the true right bank of the river. Allow four hours to reach the hut from the top of the mountain, and a further five hours from here to the road.

A well-marked track downvalley of the hut soon enters beech forest, with the usual ups and downs associated with travel in Fiordland. A terrace of celery pine and totara shrub avoids a gorge in the river, and offers some good lookouts over to yet more rocky outcrops on the Mt Titiroa ridge. Eventually, the track drops steeply to ford the middle

Morning over Fiordland, from Mt Titiroa

Granite boulder fields on Mt Titiroa

branch of Borland Burn; note that the walkwires marked on some maps no longer exist over the middle or south branches of the river, which could become impassable during heavy rain.

About 10 minutes after this crossing, a clearing and fireplace are reached, with a large, comfortable bivvy rock behind, complete with a wooden platform for up to 10 people. About 45 minutes further down the valley, the south branch creek can either be forded near the confluence or crossed via a new bridge a little way upstream. From here, the track continues easily along the main river terrace to come out directly opposite Borland Lodge, an outdoor centre run by the Southland Youth Adventure Trust, with backpacker accommodation conveniently available. Taxis, or a shuttlebus service from the main highway, should be arranged beforehand.

Green Lake/Hunter Mts

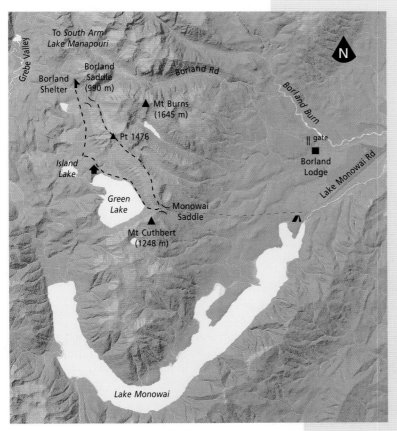

Duration: 2 days.

Grade: Moderate.

Time: 10.5 hours total. Borland Saddle to Green Lake via the tops: 7 hours. Green Lake to Borland Saddle: 3.5 hours.

Map: Hunter Mountains C44.

Access: Turn onto Borland Road from SH 99, near Blackmount, 60 km south of Te Anau.

Alternative Routes: Green Lake can be reached directly from Lake Monowai via a forest track over Monowai Saddle (allow about 6 hours).

Information: DoC Te Anau, Ph 03 249 7924. For current road conditions along Borland Road, contact Borland Lodge, Ph 03 225 5464.

WARNING! The Borland Road is often kept locked during the winter months, owing to landslips or snowfalls; check with the warden at Borland Lodge or DoC Te Anau if you are in doubt. Note also that Hiking New Zealand, a commercial guiding company, uses the tramp described throughout the summer on a regular basis. It is therefore best to avoid the lakeshore on Tuesday nights unless you are looking for company.

The Hunter Mountains stretch southwards from Lake Manapouri and lead into an area well off the beaten Fiordland track. Nestled towards the southern end of this range, high above the protective curve of Lake Monowai, lies Green Lake, a tranquil jewel set among steeply clad slopes of beech forest. Thanks to the construction of the Manapouri power scheme in the 1970s, an ECNZ access road parallels the power lines that march across this rugged landscape, carrying electricity from the West Arm generating station to the energy-hungry aluminium smelter at Tiwai Point. The unsealed Borland Road climbs steeply through the Hunter Mountains via the 1000-metre Borland Saddle, and allows for easy entry into what would otherwise be a relatively remote region of South Fiordland. This trip offers a rich variety of landscapes, from tussock-covered and rocky ridgetops to lush Fiordland beech forest, all feasible within a weekend.

The unsealed ECNZ road to Borland Saddle is narrow and winding, so drive it slowly and steadily, and be prepared to meet oncoming vehicles. Leave your car on the saddle at 990 metres, as this provides a good starting point for a trip that reaches a maximum elevation of 1645 metres. Steps lead up from the lay-by into a short section of beech forest; look out here for the strawberry fungus *(Cyttaria nigra)*, a parasite on these trees. The track soon emerges onto open tussock tops, which are followed via an indistinct trail to a series of small tarns.

Green Lake, Fiordland National Park

The ridgetop is exposed to all the weather this part of New Zealand can throw at it, and snow usually lingers on its highest sections well into summer. Being relatively low compared with much of the country further north, this ridge presents no mountaineering problems, and even the hour's side trip to the top of Mt Burns is no more than a rocky scramble.

Weave your way around these tarns to where the slope steepens. The best approach for tackling the climb ahead is directly up this ridge. Pt 1476 is reached after about two to three hours from the Borland Saddle.

On a clear day this summit offers spectacular views over Green Lake far below and to remote Fiordland mountains stretching westwards. The south coast of New Zealand, with Stewart Island suspended hazily on the horizon, is visible from this high vantage point, while eastwards, gentle farmland contrasts dramatically with the vistas in other directions. It was from this ridge that one of the largest recorded landslides in the world occurred. Look down over the rugged country around Island Lake to the west and you will see that these forest-cloaked hillocks were in fact formed by what must have been a spectacular avalanche issuing from the western slopes of the Hunter Mountains above. Towards the end of the last glacial period, an estimated 27 cubic kilometres of material slumped into the broad Grebe Valley.

A steep descent off this top leads to a perfect lunchtime tarn, shallow enough for a tempting dip on a warm day. A short distance beyond the tarn a marker pole points to a possible steep descent to Green Lake, a sensible choice if the weather is closing in over the exposed tops. In spring, look out for the local mountain buttercup, *Ranunculus buchananii*, which clings precariously to the scree slopes below the main ridge.

In good weather, stay high to enjoy the broad, undulating ridge along which the track wanders. Step carefully over this fragile terrain to avoid trampling the mosses, cushion plants and other delicate yet hardy alpine species. On exceptionally clear days, the unmistakable snowy forms of Mts Tutoko and Madeline rise up on the northern horizon near Milford Sound, while further to the northeast Mts Earnslaw and Aspiring can also be discerned.

Eventually, the ridge drops, via a conveniently angled side valley, to a boggy saddle separating Lake Monowai from Green Lake (the descent directly from Pt 1411 is a bit of a knee-wrecker). From the saddle, a track angles down through forest to the tranquil shores of Green Lake. Skirt the stony beach of the lake to reach a small A-frame shelter (six berths, wood stove and nearby toilet), which provides a wet-weather refuge; otherwise, camping on the beach is a more rewarding experience.

Crested grebes frequent this high lake, which in springtime is studded with rich clusters of the Mount Cook buttercup *(Ranunculus lyallii)*, giving way later in the season to a profusion of *Celmisia* daisy species that provide a perfect foreground to the tranquil waters beyond. Green Lake's mountain waters are cold, but on a hot afternoon, after you have built up a sweat walking over the tops, they provide a memorable place for a refreshing dip; ripples from the bathers fan out to disturb an otherwise

Slopes around Green Lake covered in mountain buttercups

balanced reflection of the forested ridges beyond.

The well-marked track back to Borland Road starts behind the hut and plunges directly into delightfully open mountain beech forest, draped in the usual accompaniment of lichens, mosses and ferns. Climb steadily to a low saddle before dropping to within sight of Island Lake. This forest walk is punctuated by a series of waist-high tussock basins, where the occasional marker defines a vague track across these contrasting grasslands before it re-enters the shady forest once more. Here you are walking over debris from the giant landslide, although nowadays the higher elevations are completely covered with beech trees, while only tussock grasses can survive on the low-lying marshy basins.

After some three hours of gentle tramping a small hut at the end of a side road is reached, from where a 25-minute walk up the switchbacks leads you back to the Borland Saddle and the start of the trip.

Trampers at a tarn above Green Lake

South Coast Track

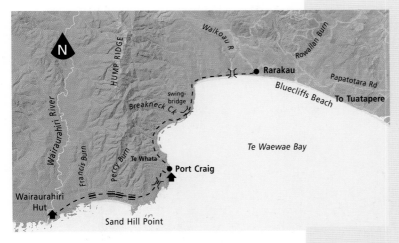

Duration: 2–3 days.

Grade: Moderate.

Time: 9–13 hours total. Rarakau carpark to Port Craig Hut (sleeps 15–20, wood stove): 5–6 hours (via inland track: 6–7 hours). Port Craig to Wairaurahiri Hut (12 bunks): 4–6 hours.

Maps: Port Craig C46, Fiordland Parkmap 273/03.

Access: From Tuatapere, take the Papatotara road to Bluecliffs Beach (28 km). Cars can be parked (at owner's risk) above the beach opposite Rarakau Station homestead.

Alternative Routes: The Tuatapere Hump Ridge Track is a privately operated 53-km, 3-day round trip, which also starts at Bluecliffs Beach. Bookings are essential (Ph/fax 03 226 6739).

Information: Tuatapere Information Centre, Ph 03 226 6399; DoC Invercargill, Ph 03 214 4589; DoC Te Anau, Ph 03 249 7924.

WARNING! Sections of this trip can be affected by the tides. Deduct 2 hours 20 minutes from the Bluff tides for those at Port Craig.

The Waitutu area of Southland offers some challenging tramping through dense tracts of lowland podocarp forests and along wild stretches of rugged coastline, with only the Southern Ocean beyond. These forests and shorelines provided a rich source of food for early Maori who visited and settled in this area. Europeans saw the economic potential in the majestic podocarp forests, and in the 1920s Port Craig, at the western end of Te Waewae Bay, was the site of the largest and most modern sawmill in the country. Relics of these earlier phases of occupation exist to this day, with Maori middens buried among the sand dunes and large wooden viaducts carrying derelict tramlines across deep ravines.

A three-day journey through this unique part of Southern Fiordland can be linked up with a jetboat trip up the Wairaurahiri River to Lake Hauroko on the return. Otherwise, it is necessary to head back along the same, or a similar, route to Bluecliffs Beach.

The newly upgraded South Coast Track starts 150 metres east of the carpark at the Rarakau Station homestead and follows along the top of an escarpment above the beach for about two kilometres. At low to mid-tide, take off your boots and walk barefoot along the sandy beach to the cluster of cribs at the Waikoau rivermouth, avoiding the ankle-twisting boulder banks that lie above the smooth sand. Note that Te Waewae Bay has a large tidal range from east to west – Port Craig is 2 hours 20 minutes ahead of Bluff.

The Waikoau River can either be waded, or crossed on a wooden footbridge, to

Crown fern and rimu forest, Waitutu

pick up the old road or beach beyond the cribs. This is private land, so travel through here with respect for the owners. It is a further three kilometres to the end of Bluecliffs Beach, where the old logging road leads into the forest and after a kilometre crosses a bridge over Track Burn. This is the boundary with Fiordland National Park, and a DoC sign marks the start of the track to Port Craig.

The route plunges abruptly into majestic stands of, predominantly, podocarp trees, consisting mainly of rimu as well as miro, totara, rata and beech. Carpets of crown ferns *(Blechnum discolor)* smother the forest floor either side of the well-benched track, which after two-and-a-half kilometres crosses Flat Creek via a long swingbridge.

The track continues mostly along the beach, with two short sections over headlands, for a further two kilometres to reach Breakneck Creek, where there is a choice of routes depending on tides or preference. The all-tide route continues inland on the true right bank of the creek, while another track leads down to a small bay. The tides need to be low and the seas not too rough for a safe trip along this beautiful coastal section, which is followed for about two hours until the inland track is rejoined. It is suggested that a 60-metre width of beach is showing before you embark on this coastal route, as there is no access to the inland track until you reach Te Whata (unnamed on the topographic map). Remember also that travel along this stretch will be a lot more relaxing if you know the tide is going out.

This coastal route offers some great rock-hopping along the wave-cut platform, interspersed with delightful stretches of white sand and plenty of clear rockpools to fossick among if time allows. Suspended on the horizon to the southeast is the purple outline of Stewart Island, frequently with its head in the clouds, while the smaller kakapo sanctuary of Codfish Island can be discerned just off the main island.

The seas off the south coast of New Zealand teem with wildlife; look out for Hector's dolphins playing in the surf, fur seals basking on the rocks and occasional Fiordland crested penguins. At certain times in the summer months, an almost unbelievable number of sooty shearwaters sweep and dive in great black clouds over the seafood-rich waters just offshore.

After two hours of travel along this interesting shoreline, the track once again heads inland, just beyond some unusual rock formations, to avoid an impassable section of coast. This inland diversion is well signposted and involves a steep scramble back up to the inland track. After another hour or so the old schoolhouse at Port Craig is reached, now converted into a comfortable tramper's hut (sleeps 15–20, wood stove). As this building is of high historic interest, please treat it with respect and carry out all rubbish.

Along the track down to the coast are plenty of old, rusting relics from the area's logging heydays. In particular, the crumbling remains of the once bustling jetty stand testament to the economic uncertainties involved in such a remote area. Nearby is a cosy sea cave connecting two small beaches; this provides a memorable shelter, with the sound of the waves breaking on either side and the chance to watch Hector's dolphins playing in the surf.

Bluecliffs Beach, Te Waewae Bay

Percy Burn Viaduct, Waitutu

Port Craig was a thriving logging town in the 1920s and 1930s, when a sizeable part of its population was involved in the extraction of timber from the virgin podocarp forests that stretched west along the coast. In order to bring up to 1800 cubic metres of timber per month back to the wharf at Port Craig, a tramway was constructed almost as far as the Wairaurahiri River, involving the building of several very impressive wooden viaducts to carry the tramlines across deep ravines.

The South Coast Track utilises this old tramway through the forest. Although it is frequently rather muddy, the path is well graded for the next 15 kilometres almost as far as the Wairaurahiri River. The solid tramline sleepers, evenly spaced along embankments and cuttings on the track, have survived to the present day and can be regarded as either help or hindrance, depending on the length of your stride. Either way, they stop the track through the regenerating manuka scrub from becoming a total quagmire, even if this does not seem to be the case after heavy rain.

Three kilometres from the Port Craig Hut a sign marks the boundary between the public Waitutu Forest and the private Rowallan Maori land, which extends all the way to the Wairaurahiri River. There is no public access down to the coast along here, and the area around Sand Hill Point is wahi tapu.

Further along the track, four massive viaducts span deep little side ravines. The Percy Burn Viaduct is the largest of these at a length of 125 metres and a height of 36 metres above the creekbed. It was extensively repaired by the Southland Port Craig Viaduct Trust in 1994, which took care to match their modern additions with the original Australian hardwood construction. The three other viaducts encountered have also been redecked and rendered safe for trampers.

Towards the end of the four- to five-hour tramp from Port Craig, the tramline comes to an end and the track once again enters mature, uncut forest for the final drop down three river terraces to the 12-bunk Wairaurahiri Hut. On the other side of the river is the privately run Waitutu Lodge, which provides alternative accommodation with hot showers; a warden is in residence here at all times.

A pre-arranged pick-up by jetboat from here can whisk you up the Wairaurahiri River into Lake Hauroko, a journey of about one-and-a-half hours. Wairaurahiri Wilderness Jet operates this service on demand and will also take you back to your car at Bluecliffs Beach, an hour from the lake. This return completes an excellent circuit of a unique section of coastal Fiordland without the need to backtrack at all.

The full South Coast Track continues on an increasingly rough trail for another 26 kilometres beyond the Wairaurahiri River as far as Big River, where the official route finishes; beyond here is a true wilderness experience best left to the purists.